Early Childhood Quality Rating Scale—Emergent Curriculum (ECQRS-EC)

Kathy Sylva Iram Siraj Brenda Taggart Denise Kingston

Published by Teachers College Press, 1234 Amsterdam Avenue, New York, NY 10027

ISBN No. 978-0-80778655-0

Front cover photos by: FatCamera, Stella E, polplasen, and Halfpoint, all via iStock by Getty Images.

Printed on acid-free paper
Manufactured in the United States of America
22 21 20 19 18 17 16 15 14 13 12 11 10 9 8 7 6 5 4 3 2 1

About the Authors

Kathy Sylva is Professor of Educational Psychology at the University of Oxford. She has researched extensively in the education and care of young children, with a special interest in the effects of early education and also the role of education in combating social disadvantage.

Iram Siraj is Professor of Child Development and Education at the University of Oxford. She is coauthor of each of the Curriculum, Leadership and Interaction Quality Rating Scales (CLIQRS) and has led several RCTs on effective professional learning.

Brenda Taggart is an Honorary Senior Research Associate at University College London Institute of Education. She co-led on the Effective Pre-school, Primary, and Secondary Education Project (EPPSE 1997–2014). Her background is in teaching and research that explores the impact of educational initiatives.

Denise Kingston is Senior Researcher at Oxford University and an Honorary Research Fellow at the University of Sussex. She is a specialist in children's development, with a background in educational psychology. Her research focus is effective professional development and EC pedagogy and practice.

Acknowledgments

We are indebted to the children, families, and early years centers who participated in the Effective Pre-school, Primary, and Secondary Education Project (EPPSE 1997–2014). This publication arose from the detailed observations conducted in early years centers as part of this research.

In addition, we would like to thank the many researchers, analysts, and policymakers who worked with us for more than 20 years on EPPSE. We have benefited from their insights, and without their help and collaboration, the research would not have had the global impact it has attained.

As the original pioneers of observation rating scales, we also owe a debt of gratitude to Thelma Harms, Richard M. Clifford, and Debby Cryer of the Frank Porter Graham Child Development Center at the University of North Carolina. Their work has inspired researchers from around the world to look closely at early years environments and the vital role that adults have in improving education and care for our youngest children.

Contents

Foreword

With record high percentages of young children now in preschool classrooms and a growing international commitment to providing universal preschool education, systematic attention to classroom quality is needed as never before. Yet, numerous studies have found the tools the field uses to assess and support quality to be lacking, and a recent National Academies of Sciences, Engineering, and Medicine report has questioned the curriculum approaches most widely used in the United States (National Academies of Sciences, Engineering, and Medicine, 2024). Fortunately, the new evidence-based tool described in this volume, the Early Childhood Quality Rating Scale—Emergent Curriculum (ECQRS-EC), is now available to assess pedagogy and practice with particular attention to intentional supports for emergent academic skills in literacy, mathematics, and science. It also explicitly assesses practices supporting diversity and inclusion.

The ECQRS-EC is firmly grounded in culturally and developmentally appropriate practice and validated by decades of research on the links between practice and both immediate and long-term academic outcomes. As part of a suite of assessment tools that includes the Sustained Shared Thinking and Emotional Well-Being Scale (SSTEW; Siraj et al., 2015, 2024) and the Movement Environment Rating Scale (MOVERS; Archer & Siraj, 2017, 2024), the ECQRS-EC offers a comprehensive means for individual educators, centers, and schools, and even entire systems, to assess quality. Together, these tools provide a solid foundation for a statewide Quality Rating and Improvement System or other continuous improvement systems, including, we suggest, Head Start as part of professional development and the Designation Renewal System. We know this tool is being used as such in a number of other countries.

The authors of the ECQRS-EC are distinguished researchers whose knowledge and expertise are built on theory, research, and deep engagement with practice and respect for early educators. Not as well known in the United States as it ought to be, their work over more than two decades in the practices that enhance learning, development, and well-being to produce persistent, long-term gains for young children and reduce later educational inequalities has been groundbreaking (see, e.g., Sylva et al., 2004). This rigorous research on the links between specific practices and children's academic success validates the items that constitute the ECQRS-EC and the instrument as a whole. Research that has worldwide significance is rare, but these authors have strong credentials from decades of work on projects that have global relevance for early years research, policy, and practice.

The two of us have worked to support evidence-based policy and practice in early childhood education for more than 40 years. We began this work at the HighScope Educational Research Foundation, where Steve conducted the first comprehensive benefit–cost analysis of the Perry Preschool study and Ellen co-developed a large-scale teacher professional development initiative aimed at producing the kind of quality that the Perry Preschool had demonstrated could change lives.

As co-directors of the National Institute for Early Education Research, we have seen tremendous progress in public programs since then, but less than we would have hoped with respect to quality. Our subsequent work developing and using observational tools to assess and improve preschool quality convinces us that the ECQRS-EC can be an effective tool to support professional development and quality improvement and to improve accountability (not individually, but collectively). The current body of classroom quality observation tools lacks a focused assessment of emergent skills across literacy, mathematics, and science.

Using the ECQRS-EC as a teacher self-assessment tool would be extremely effective for ensuring that teachers understand the intentional pedagogical strategies that enhance learning in these foundational skills for educational success. Large-scale use in state and other continuous improvement systems can help to provide all children with the early childhood education each needs to thrive.

W. Steven Barnett
Senior Co-Director, National Institute for Early Education Research &
Board of Governors Professor, Rutgers, The State University of New Jersey

Ellen C. Frede
Senior Co-Director, National Institute for Early Education Research &
Research Professor, Rutgers, The State University of New Jersey

References

Archer, C., & Siraj, I. (2017). *Movement Environment Rating Scale (MOVERS) for 2–6-year-olds provision: Improving physical development through movement and physical activity.* Trentham Books & UCL-IoE Press.

Archer, C., & Siraj, I. (2024). *Movement Environment Rating Scale (MOVERS): Supporting physical development and movement play in early childhood.* Routledge.

National Academies of Sciences, Engineering, and Medicine. (2024). *A new vision for high-quality preschool curriculum.* The National Academies Press. https://doi.org/10.17226/27429

Siraj, I., & Kingston, D. (in press). *The Pedagogical Leadership in the Early Years (PLEY) Scale.* Routledge.

Siraj, I., Kingston, D., & Melhuish, E. (2024). *The Sustained Shared Thinking and Emotional Well-Being (SSTEW) Scale: Supporting process quality in early childhood.* Routledge.

Sylva, K., Melhuish, E., Sammons, P., Siraj, I., & Taggart, B. (2004). *The Effective Provision of Pre-School Education (EPPE) Project: Findings from pre-school to end of key stage 1.* Retrieved May 4, 2024, from https://dera.ioe.ac.uk/id/eprint/18189/2/SSU-SF-2004-01.pdf

Introduction to the Early Childhood Quality Rating Scale—Emergent Curriculum (ECQRS-EC)

ECQRS-EC is a quality rating scale that can be used for research, self-evaluation, improvement, audit, and regulation. The ECQRS-EC builds on the Early Childhood Environment Rating Scale—Extension (ECERS-E; Sylva et al., 2003/2011), which was designed to be used with the Early Childhood Environment Rating Scale—Revised (ECERS-R; Harms et al., 2004). It was developed for the Effective Provision of Pre-school Education Project (EPPE). As the children in the study got older, the project morphed into the Effective Pre-school, Primary and Secondary Education Project (EPPSE/EPPE 1997–2014; see IOE—Faculty of Education, 2024, for publications). EPPSE was a large-scale longitudinal study funded by the UK government to investigate effective provision in early years education and care. The project, along with an associate study, Researching Effective Pedagogy in the Early Years (REPEY; Siraj-Blatchford et al., 2002), has been highly influential in transforming both practice and policy in the UK and abroad. EPPSE went beyond the simple question "What are the effects of early education?" to explore whether the effects lasted over time and their impact on children with different background demographics.

The use of rating scales goes back to 1982 with the development of observational scales by researchers at the Frank Porter Graham Child Development Center at the University of North Carolina. The most widely used was the Early Childhood Environment Rating Scale—Revised (ECERS-R; Harms et al., 2004; now ECERS-3; Harms et al., 2014), which focused on environmental quality—including those spatial, programmatic, and interpersonal features that directly affect the children aged 3–5 years old—in early years centers. The scope of the US observation rating scales has expanded over many years to include scales that focus on the environment for infants/toddlers (ITERS-3; Harms et al., 2017), school-aged (5–12 years) care (SACERS-R; Harms et al., 2015), and family day care (FCCERS-3; Harms et al., 2019).

Since the turn of the century, there has been an increasing global awareness of the importance of high-quality early years experiences for improving children's later academic, emotional, behavioral, and physical outcomes (Burchinal et al., 2002; Melhuish et al., 2015). This period also saw a rapid increase in the numbers of children looked after in center-based care and education. During the first decades of the 21st century, a great deal has been learned about those elements of the early years environment that lead to better experiences and outcomes for children. There has been a wealth of large-scale international research studies (Burger, 2010; Huang & Siraj, 2023; Magnuson et al., 2016; Melhuish et al., 2015; OECD, 2022; Siraj et al., 2023; Sylva et al., 2020; Thorpe et al., 2020) with remarkably similar findings that point to the pivotal role of adults working with young children to support the development of the skills and abilities needed to be competent learners in the 21st century (Sylva et al., 2020).

The early years are no longer seen as simply a preparation for school, but as a unique phase of development that demands skilled educators who understand both child development as well as developmentally appropriate practice. It is this increasing emphasis on what practitioners *do* (pedagogy) and not only *what they offer* (resources, timetables, routines) that has been the driving force in the development of a new family of rating scales.

The ECQRS-EC is included in the family of the Curriculum, Leadership and Interaction Quality Rating Scales (CLIQRS), which includes the Sustained Shared Thinking and Emotional Well-Being Scale (SSTEW; Siraj et al., 2015, 2024), the Movement Environment Rating Scale (MOVERS; Archer & Siraj, 2017, 2024), and the Pedagogical Leadership in the Early Years Scale (PLEY; Siraj & Kingston, 2025). Taken together, this family of scales covers key components of children's development: academic, social–emotional, and physical. These are underpinned by the PLEY Scale with its strong focus on pedagogical leadership within early years centers. Research has shown a clear relationship between successful leadership and educational effectiveness (Day & Sammons, 2020; Leithwood, 2017; Sammons et al., 2011; Walker & Hallinger, 2015). Delivering high-quality learning experiences to children demands skilled educators in centers where there is a vision, effective teamwork, and good communication. High-quality leadership paves the road to success.

Increasingly, globalization has shown that those who contribute the most to the global economy and their own well-being are those who are literate, numerate, and emotionally well grounded with curious minds that will sustain them as confident and well-rounded learners. These are the skills—alongside the abilities to work as part of a team, possess high self-regulation, be flexible in new situations, and exhibit social awareness—that are essential for successful citizenship in the 21st century. Using all the scales in the CLIQRS family will help educators to develop a more holistic approach to the development of their children and their center. Used together, these tools shine a light on what quality looks like for the academic, social–behavioral, well-being, and physical development of children underpinned by good practice in leadership.

All the scales in the CLIQRS family recognize the vital role of developmentally appropriate pedagogy that brings the curriculum alive each day. The CLIQRS scales have a particular focus on process and pedagogy as well as structural and environmental quality, hence the move away from the term "environment rating scales" to "quality rating scales."

Young children's learning depends on a wide range of experiences that support their holistic development. There is broad global agreement that communication, language, literacy, numeracy, understanding of science, physical development, and personal, social, and emotional development are important curriculum domains. Whereas the English curriculum is structured by these "domains of development," the curriculum in some other countries is structured by "experiences" needed for successful development. The Norwegian curriculum (Norway Ministry of Education and Research, 2023), for example, states that all children should be offered experiences to care for their surroundings and their natural environment. Moreover, in Norway, children themselves have a legal right to participate in discussions concerning their daily life in the kindergarten.

Despite many differences in curricular frameworks around the world, there is increasing agreement that the emerging skills of language and literacy, mathematics, and science should be supported by playful pedagogy in the early years. These emerging skills can be found in those national curricula structured around developmental domains as well as those based on experiences that all children should have.

In devising the ECQRS-EC, we have used research evidence on how educators can effectively support language and emergent literacy, emergent mathematics, and science rather than basing it on existing curricula or guidance. As a result, the items and indicators do not always align with various government policies and their associated curriculum guidance. Credit for various steps in the quality incline of this scale has been based on a large research literature and on the experiences of professionals and experts in the field whom we have worked with for many years.

The ECQRS-EC provides centers with a means to assess pedagogy and curriculum designed to support aspects of intellectual development we call "academic." It covers areas of the emerging curriculum in preschool: language and literacy, mathematics, and science, together with a subscale on supporting and planning for diversity and inclusion. The diversity and inclusion subscale helps ensure that early years educators plan for the needs of all individuals, always mindful of gender and cultural differences in children who are developing at different rates.

The original ECERS-E has been used in research studies (Anders et al., 2012; Hall et al., 2009; Lehrl et al., 2016; Siraj et al., 2003; Sylva et al., 2006, 2007) that have demonstrated the relationship between the quality of the early years pedagogy and environment and child outcomes. These studies have demonstrated that it is a valid and reliable instrument for assessing the quality of a center. The ECQRS-EC retains much of the ECERS-E, which was the first observational quality scale to focus directly on the development of emergent 'academic' skills in literacy, mathematics, and science. The quality items in the first ECERS-E were designed to assess those aspects of practice that research had demonstrated supported later academic outcomes. In keeping with other scales in the CLIQRS, ECQRS-EC has a stronger focus on the role of the educator, their pedagogy, and planning. Reflecting this, the ECQRS-EC has an additional Item in the Language and Emergent Literacy Subscale: "Words and Sentences" and two new Items in the Emergent Mathematics Subscale: "Math Talk and Thinking Mathematically" and "Subitizing" (answering "How many?" without counting). There is also a revised "Reading and Representing Simple Number" Item now called "Understanding and Representing Number." The Emergent Science Subscale has an additional Item called "Developing Scientific Thinking and the Scientific Method." The Diversity Subscale, now called "Supporting Diversity and Inclusion," reflects the importance of sensitivity to supporting special needs and being inclusive of all cultures, including Indigenous people.

If researchers and educators are interested in the overall development of children, then we advise that the ECQRS-EC is used alongside the SSTEW and the MOVERS to pick up on physical and social–emotional quality as well as the intellectual component.

The Underlying Principles of ECQRS-EC

The Emergent Curriculum supports the development of "emergent academic skills" and recognizes the continuity between the development of intellectual skills during the preschool period and subsequent learning of school subjects after school entry. In fact, emergent academic skills develop from birth when infants begin their visual and tactile exploration of the social, emotional, and physical world. They make mental representations of the world they encounter, and these enable them to recognize familiar persons, sounds, and smells. These representations are stored in their minds for future use and are the beginnings of each child's "mental map" of the world that they inhabit. These earliest representations are not "academic" but they are clearly intellectual, as child development theorists pointed out (Gopnik et al., 1999). The early mental representations underpin all later learning, including memory, retrieval, and noticing differences and similarities. For this reason, it is important that very early emergent skills are nurtured by sensitive adults at home and in early childhood settings.

We have used the word "academic" to refer to bodies of knowledge often called "curriculum or school subjects," for example, English (or German or Mandarin), mathematics, and science. Some educators call these "school skills," but we prefer the word academic because it is more specific than the broader set of school skills that includes listening, concentration, or getting along with peers. Developing these **emergent** skills is important in the preschool years because three decades of research have shown that these "pre-academic" skills strongly influence future reading, writing, numeracy, and understanding of science (Adams, 1990; Snow et al., 1999). Moreover, supporting emergent academic skills in the preschool period is more important for children from disadvantaged backgrounds than for children from more advantaged ones (Duncan & Magnuson, 2013; Sammons et al., 2008; Sylva et al., 2010).

By the end of the last century, researchers had identified discrete emergent skills that are acquired during the preschool period that enable children to become successful readers and writers. Marie Clay (1993) was an early pioneer in this work. She studied that period *before* formal reading instruction and discovered how children gradually map print onto the language they already know so that they can build meaning onto the text. They do this by gradually learning a host of skills that will be needed later in school to support formal instruction. These include print concepts (Clay, 1993; Justice & Ezell, 2001), alphabet knowledge (letter sounds and names; Bowman & Treiman, 2004), phonological awareness (Mann & Foy, 2003), and emergent mark making that turns into early writing (Welsch et al., 2003).

Some scholars consider oral language to be one of the emergent literacy skills (Justice & Kaderavek, 2002; Justice & Pullen, 2003) while others (Snow, 1991) view oral language skills as distinct from the skills tied directly to print. The ECQRS-EC includes items related to oral language as part of the Language and Emergent Literacy Subscale since oral language supports emergent literacy (Snow, 1991). However, we recognize that oral language begins in the first year of life and is important in its own right for communication and not only as precursor to later reading.

Not long after emergent literacy was identified in the 1990s, others began to study emergent mathematics (Nunes & Bryant, 1996) and emergent science (Agogi et al., 2014; Carey & Smith, 1993; Glauert et al., 2013). Developmental scientists and innovative teachers demonstrated through their research that the precursor skills that feed into more formal academic skills were typically acquired well before school entry; it is the goal of ECQRS-EC to assess and guide the provision in early childhood education that supports their development.

A strong foundation of pre-literacy, pre-mathematics, and pre-science during early childhood allows a smooth transition to English, mathematics, and science in the first year of school. The quality items in the first ECERS-E were designed to assess those aspects of practice that research had demonstrated supported later academic outcomes. The influential EPPSE study (Sylva et al., 2006, 2007, 2010; Taggart, 2010; Taggart et al., 2015) showed the predictive power of quality (measured via the ECERS-E) in supporting emerging academic skills that feed into later academic and social development. German researchers led by Rossbach and Anders (Anders et al., 2012, 2013) used a version of the ECERS-E in Germany, and they too found that the quality of provision for emergent academic skills predicted later school achievement.

To simplify a very complex matter, in this scale we will assume that curriculum refers to *what* we want children to learn, to those aspects of development that we believe education should encourage and support. The emergent academic curriculum refers to the knowledge and skills acquired during early childhood that will support formal school learning when the child enters education. By way of contrast, pedagogy refers to the *how* of practice, to those educational practices and physical resources that are intentionally and relationally implemented to ensure that all children achieve the goals of the curriculum. However, we recognize that academic skills are only part of the broader curriculum for the early years, which includes social, emotional, and physical development, along with dispositions. The broader curriculum can be assessed by using all the scales in the CLIQRS family.

Underlying all scales in the CLIQRS is the concept of "intentional pedagogy." Siraj et al. (2024) describe it as the deliberate implementation of the curriculum in a way that begins with each child's current development and then chooses specific interactions or resources that "encourage/extend" the child to a higher level of functioning. According to Epstein (2014), intentional pedagogy does not happen by chance.

An intentional educator

- acts with knowledge and purpose to ensure that children acquire the knowledge (content) and skills they need to succeed in the childhood center and throughout life;
- plans for all aspects of learning: child-led and adult-led sessions, learning environments inside–outside, home learning, routines, transitions, etc.;
- uses their knowledge, judgment, and expertise to organize learning experiences for all children with the right amount of challenge;
- responds when an unexpected situation arises (as it always does); they can recognize a learning opportunity and are able to take advantage of it spontaneously.

An intentional educator does not rely only on intuition or chance but plans for all aspects of learning, such as: what resources they offer and the way they organize and enhance the environment; adult-led sessions; small and/or whole group sessions where educators know what they want the children to learn (e.g., cooking or dialogic reading); inside–outside learning experiences; home learning; routines; and transitions. All the above are planned thoughtfully and purposefully, and are responsive to the needs of the children.

Intentional educators use their knowledge, judgment, and expertise to organize learning experiences that are engaging for *all* children. So, for example, when planning small group time, they plan learning opportunities that reflect children's interests and make links to the children's families, their local communities, and recent events as well as following the curriculum and ensuring progression. They design activities that offer the appropriate levels of challenge, ensuring they are neither too difficult (which could lead to frustration and giving up) or too easy (which could lead to boredom). They observe the children, assessing their progress on a minute-by-minute and daily basis and respond accordingly. For example, if the children are finding a particular puzzle too hard and tend to leave it uncompleted, they may intervene and support the children in completing it and/or replace the puzzle with an easier one, to support perseverance and maintain interest. Finally, while they do plan, they also respond intentionally when an unexpected situation arises (as they often do); they are flexible and can recognize a learning opportunity and are able to take advantage of it.

How can the observer identify intentions? This scale investigates intentional pedagogy as described above. This exploration of an educator's intent cannot always be captured easily via a purely observational scale. Some intentions can be easily observed, for instance, where an educator discusses with a child their interests and then they build on the child's interests in an observable way. They might provide toy diggers and excavators in the sand tray, and the observed language/math/investigations build on the child's experience of interacting with the educator and these tangible resources.

The intention of the educator to provide engaging learning opportunities that match a child's level of development can be observed in interactions that result in the acquisition of a new skill, as well as in conversations that scaffold learning and extend thinking (sustained shared thinking). Such interactions may be accompanied by the use of materials that pique interests and support motivation. Note that the educator's intentional strategies do not always support the child's move to the next level in their thinking because this is a complex process. However, if you see numerous failed intentions and children who are uninterested and frustrated, it is likely that either the educator is not practiced in such interactions or they do not know the children well enough, including their interests or level of development.

In some circumstances the intention of the educator is more difficult to ascertain as it is based on their professional knowledge of a particular child/group. If the observer is unsure, then it is strongly recommended that they look closely at the section called "Use of Supplementary (Nonobservation) Evidence" (page 20). It is highly recommended that observers ensure, before embarking on an observation, that they build time into their visit to look at other forms of evidence. The educator in charge of the class will also need to know before the visit that they may be asked to provide some additional information about their activities to assist the observer. Much supplemental information can be sought unobtrusively from looking closely at planning, classroom displays, and photographic records. Children's folders are another good source of supplemental information. It may be necessary, however, to ask questions of the educator about the intention of their activity or to request access to their planning/child records. This must be done sensitively, and when questioning the intention of an educator it may be more helpful to start the conversation with "I really liked the activity/interaction that you and Ben were engaged in; can you tell me a bit more about Ben and why you chose this activity?" rather than "What were your intentions when working with Ben?" For further examples of helpful questions, see the "Use of Supplementary (Nonobservation) Evidence" section (page 20).

The ECQRS-EC is scored in the same way as other scales in the CLIQRS suite of quality rating scales. It is designed to be administered in centers with children between the ages of 3 and 6 years old (up to 5 years 11 months) who are in an early childhood education and care (ECEC) facility. Although designed for children *between* the ages of 3 and 6, it is recognized that these children may be in centers that contain some children at age 2 and some at age 6. It should be noted that previous versions of the scale (ECERS-E) focused on the age range 3–5 because children in the UK enter statutory education at age 5. Now that the scale has proved its usefulness and reliability across many countries, we believe it caters for the wider age range of 3–6 years, which is common across Europe, Asia Pacific, and elsewhere.

Rationale for the Development of the New Items and Indicators in the ECQRS-EC

Since the publication of the first ECERS-E in 2003, research and practice have changed, deepened, and become more rigorous. For example, the notion of pre-literacy, especially, is already embraced by many early years educators who regularly support the development of phonological awareness and letter recognition as important and necessary precursors to learning how to read. However, phonics is not the only pre-academic literacy skill; vocabulary and understanding spoken language are as important for learning to read as letter sound knowledge.

There follows detailed description of the need recognized by the authors to add new Items to the original ECERS-E. We have also made small changes, such as minor adjustments to some Indicators to clarify their meaning, and have extended examples and supplementary information where required.

Language and Emergent Literacy

Successful reading requires bottom-up skills, which include recognizing letters and knowing their links to sounds. It also requires top-down skills, which consist of a child's prior knowledge of vocabulary and how language works (e.g., the "ed" of the past tense) and knowledge of the world (e.g., children wear pajamas for sleeping). To successfully read the word pajamas, children need the bottom-up skill that consists of the link between the initial letter "p" and its sound. However, top-down skills would enable the child to use information earlier or later in the sentence about children getting ready for bed. So, the real-world knowledge of clothes we wear to bed can help a child to read the word "pajamas." There is debate about the role of bottom-up versus top-down skills when learning to read, but the international literature suggests that skilled readers need both, especially in a language such as English, which is so irregular compared to languages such as Spanish or Welsh.

Item 7: Words and Sentences

The new Item 7 focuses on adult strategies related to introducing new words and encouraging children to use conventional forms of speech, such as "ed" for past tense and "s" for plurals. When children do not use conventional forms of speech, credit in Item 7 is given to the adults modeling the conventional form without implying disapproval of what the child has just said. Revisions to the Language and Emergent Literacy Subscale have been based on recent research (such as Masters et al., 2023) that identified specific early childhood education activities for building vocabulary.

Countries around the world have different policies for the age at which children begin formal reading instruction, with the UK as one of the earliest. Its children begin formal reading instruction in the reception class, a year when many of the children have not yet reached the age of 5. Practice is very different in many Scandinavian countries, which delay the start of reading instruction until children are at least 6 years old.

However, we have used the evidence base related to how educators can effectively support emergent literacy, mathematics, and science while devising the content of ECQRS-EC, rather than looking at existing curricula or guidance. As a result, the contents of our scale do not always align with various government policies and their associated curriculum guidance. What we suggest is designed for use in early childhood centers wishing to support children's development and learning through a playful intentional pedagogy.

Changes to and Additional Items in Emergent Mathematics

Revised ECERS-E Item 8 Now ECQRS-EC Item 9
Understanding and representing number

In the original ECERS-E, Item 8 was called "Reading and Representing Simple Numbers" and its content focused on children learning to recognize and reproduce written numerals. These are abstract representations and due to their symbolic nature, young children often find them difficult to understand. Many mathematicians suggest that other representations, including concrete and pictorial, should be used in conjunction with or even before introducing numerals (e.g., Clements & Sarama, 2014; Merttens, 2012). For this reason, other representations have been added to this Item, and it is now called "Understanding and Representing Number" (now Item 9).

Van de Walle et al. (2018) suggested that moving between and within different mathematical representations, including giving the math a meaningful context, engaging in math talk where children explain and describe the math they are doing, and using concrete, pictorial, and abstract (CPA) representations improves children's understanding and supports the retention of new mathematical ideas. The new Item 9 incorporates context, math talk, and CPA representations, and focuses on learning mathematics with understanding.

Item 10: Math Talk and Thinking Mathematically

Item 10 is a new Item that, first, reflects the importance of children understanding that mathematics is real, interesting, and relevant to them, as it encourages them to think and talk about their mathematical understandings using real-life, meaningful contexts; second, the Item recognizes the fundamental role of language and how the educator supports children to develop their mathematical vocabulary as well as to be able to talk about/show their mathematical thinking, sometimes called "math talk." During math talk children are encouraged to engage in mathematical reasoning and problem solving to represent their ideas. Children are asked to explain their mathematical thinking with questions like these: How did you do that/know? What are you planning? What is the pattern? How did you get your answer? Is there another way? Children may answer using concrete objects, drawings, and/or talk. Answering such questions strengthens and deepens children's understanding of mathematics, as they reason (and explain their thinking) and problem solve (observe, form, or recognize the problem [what question is being asked]), make predictions, test out solutions, and evaluate or reflect on what they have done.

Item 11c: Subitizing

Item 11c: Subitizing (answering "How many?" without counting) is the ability to instantly recognize a collection of objects without counting (e.g., as children do when playing games using dice). Subitizing is an important mathematical skill that children are born with and that develops through exposure and experience over time.

Children begin with **perceptual subitizing**, which involves instantly recognizing a small collection of objects, without thinking or counting.

Then they move on to **conceptual subitizing,** which involves seeing patterns in different arrangements of objects and combining them. This is still fairly instantaneous as it does not involve counting (sees and describes 5 objects as a collection of 2 and 3, or 4 and 1).

The ability to subitize is an important part of developing a strong mathematical foundation and understanding of number (Baroody, 1987). Reys et al. (2012) suggest subitizing can save time, consolidate, and support the development of more elaborate counting skills and quicken the process of learning how to calculate. Subitizing saves children time when answering "How many?" as children see quantities in groups and do not need to revert to counting objects one by one. This is particularly useful later when children are dealing with more complex numbers or beginning to calculate.

Some examples of the usefulness of subitizing over time follow. Example 1 shows how subitizing supports children in developing more complex number and counting skills. Children who can subitize small groups are able to develop their counting skills by beginning their counting after the subitized group.

> **Example 1:** Children who can subitize 5, including 5 fingers, will look at 7 fingers and recognize one hand as 5  and be able to say 5, then count on the remaining 2 fingers  —5, 6, 7—without needing to count each finger individually.
>
> **Example 2:** When asked to calculate 7 + 8, a child may visualize the amounts or work with a partner, each holding up their fingers to represent the numbers 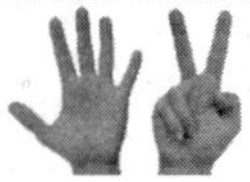 and 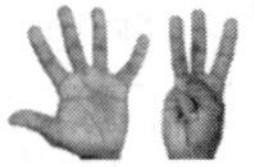 and quickly see that 7 + 8 consists of double 7 and 1 more. The child may know that double 7 is 14, so 7 + 8 must be 14 and 1 more, which is 15.

It is interesting to note that before children know the words or symbols for numbers, they acquire an approximate number system (ANS), which enables them to approximate the magnitude of a group without relying on language or symbols. Even 6-month-old babies can compare groups of objects and recognize when the number of objects changes. Introducing language, such as asking children to make comparisons and identify which group has more or less, for example, links language to the ANS (see Item 11b: Sorting, Matching, and Comparing). So too does subitizing (see Item 11c), answering "How many?" without counting, which is the ability to instantly recognize a collection of objects without counting, e.g., knowing they have been given three sweets or knowing the amount of dots on a dice without needing to count.

In conclusion, supporting children's natural propensity to subitize provides meaningful experiences, which promote early understanding of number and quantity. It supports the building of connections between numbers and quantities, which enables children to think flexibly about them. It builds visual number sense, which increases children's abilities to form mental images of quantities. This allows children to manipulate numbers in their heads, which, in turn, gives them a strong sense of reference for mathematical problem-solving situations such as estimation, measurement, and different forms of calculation. Not all educators feel confident teaching math; if you lack knowledge in this area, we recommend some of the readings in the References section to support understanding (e.g., Clements & Sarama, 2017/2019; Reys et al., 2012).

Emergent Science

Item 14: Developing Scientific Thinking and the Scientific Process

The need for an additional item in the Emergent Science Subscale is to encourage the development of early years scientific thinking and reflects research undertaken in this area since the publication of the original ECERS-E. Of particular note is the Creative Little Scientists (CLS) study undertaken in nine European countries (Glauert et al., 2013; Rossis & Stylianidou 2014). Relevant to the ECQRS-EC, the CLS study emphasizes fostering young children's interests and motivation to lead them into scientific understanding, and how educators manage this in a creative way through everyday activities.

Fundamental to the development of young children's scientific thinking is how they are supported in growing their curiosity and enquiring minds. This is the basis of inquiry-based science education, which opens the door to a wider knowledge and understanding of science content and the development of scientific process skills. Inquiry-based science education, far from being at odds with play, can enhance a child's play experience by embedding play-based learning.

While the original ECERS-E focused on provision for science exploration and the educator's role in questioning, the new Item extends this by providing insights into how educators capitalize on a child's curiosity and channel this into embracing the scientific methods of observing materials/phenomena, asking enquiring questions, developing hypotheses, testing, and reflection/reporting on results. It extends the existing items in the ECERS-E, which has a stronger focus on the resources available (both living and nonliving) in an early years center to stimulate scientific inquiry.

When scoring Item 14, credit is given in an incremental way to reflect steps in the scientific process (observing, questioning, hypothesizing, testing, recording, and discussing results). It also relates to the adult's intentional pedagogy in using child-initiated or routine activities to guide children through the scientific process. The lowest score is given if staff do not encourage questioning and curiosity. A minimal score suggests adults acknowledge children's questions and use routine activities to pique children's interest. For good practice, staff must intentionally use child-initiated or routine activities to help children develop meaningful questions leading to a hypothesis that could reasonably be answered/investigated. The highest scores are awarded if staff help children to investigate (test) their hypothesis. With older children the observer should look for evidence that the results of an investigation have been recorded and discussed, as this can provide opportunities for further questioning/investigations. If the observer does not see this on the day, they should look for evidence either in displays, in lesson plans, or by questioning the adult. The recording of investigation is not required for the youngest children.

The Overlap Between the Sustained Shared Thinking and Emotional Well-Being Scale (SSTEW) and Mathematics and Science Items in ECQRS-EC

The starting point in the new Emergent Science Item is the extent to which the adult stimulates a discussion with a child/group of children through sensitive questioning. Questioning, in this context, is a device to extend children's thinking, leading to a deeper and more complex conversation. The Researching Effective Pedagogy in the Early Years (REPEY; Siraj-Blatchford et al., 2002) study highlighted the importance of the frequency of high-quality adult/child verbal interactions, which were more frequently seen in centers that scored higher in quality on the ECERS-E scale. Children in these centers also had better long-term outcomes. During the REPEY research, the researchers reported on adult/child interactions, which were used by the adult as an opportunity to work together with the child in an intellectual way to solve a problem, clarify a concept, evaluate activities, or extend a narrative. Both parties contributed to the thinking, and the conversation was developed and extended. In REPEY, this was referred to as "sustained shared thinking" and was the inspiration for the SSTEW scale (Siraj et al., 2015), which has also been revised (Siraj et al., 2024).

The SSTEW quality rating scale extends REPEY's original focus on effective pedagogy into a deeper understanding of what contributes to children's learning, social–emotional development, and well-being. Items in the SSTEW delve into how children are supported in developing their critical thinking, curiosity, and problem solving. There is, therefore, some overlap between SSTEW and this scale, in terms of both academic learning and being sensitive and responsive to children, which is known to support their social–emotional development and well-being (Siraj-Blatchford et al., 2002). The SSTEW refers to "Practices that support emotional development and also task focus in problem-solving all rest on communication between adult and child. Narrative is important here but so too is guided thinking based on open questions and sharing of views" (Siraj et al., 2024).

The use by adults of open-ended, sensitive questioning can lead children to problem solve and find things out, neither of which is confined solely to scientific inquiry. Getting children to observe, make guesses, and then test out their ideas is fundamental to many areas of exploration. In the ECQRS-EC, this is evident in the overlap between pedagogical practices to support the development of science and mathematical reasoning as they are both inextricably linked to problem solving and finding out. For instance, a typical problem-solving strategy (see Mayer & Wittrock

1996) includes splitting the problem up into its component aspects (e.g., What information do we have? What further information might we need? What do we want to find out? And/or, what possible solutions would work?)

Problem-solving competence is multidimensional: It can be interdisciplinary, as well as domain specific (Klieme et al., 2001). It should also be noted that problem solving may also be part of social reasoning (e.g., see HighScope's [2018] six steps to conflict resolution) as well as mathematical (e.g., word or story problems) and scientific (e.g., close observation followed by hypothesis testing) reasoning. Reasoning and problem solving, therefore, occur in SSTEW as well as in both the Mathematics and Science Subscales of the ECQRS-EC.

Given the above, it is unsurprising that the Items on Math Talk and Thinking Mathematically and Developing Scientific Thinking and the Scientific Process overlap, as they both encompass how adults develop children's curiosity and problem-solving abilities.

The importance of reasoning and problem solving within the ECQRS-EC reflects current thinking about the skills children need to develop for the 21st century (World Economic Forum, 2016). As well as important literacies (including literacy, numeracy, scientific literacy, and cultural and civic literacy) and character qualities (such as curiosity, initiative, persistence, and cultural awareness), the World Economic Forum identified four competencies: Critical Thinking and Problem Solving, Creativity, Communication, and Collaboration. Activities that support reasoning and problem solving give children the opportunity to communicate what they see and think. They afford opportunities for children to work together and learn collaboratively. Supporting children to ask questions is an essential part of critical thinking (the ability to use and question information rather than simply absorbing and then describing it). When children observe and ask questions, they show the beginning of problem solving and the scientific process; that is, they make close observations and develop their own questions and/or identify "problems" to be solved. This process—of identifying problems to be solved and asking questions that may lead to predictions or hypotheses and further investigation—is a creative process. The new Items, Math Talk and Thinking Mathematically and Developing Scientific Thinking and the Scientific Process, therefore, support the four competences identified as skills for the 21st century.

Supporting Diversity and Inclusion

The Diversity Subscale in the ECERS-E is now called the Supporting Diversity and Inclusion Subscale. There are no new Items in this Subscale. However, each Item has been revised to reflect our learning in using this Subscale over the last 20 years. The Diversity Subscale was shown in the EPPSE study to correlate with the highest outcomes for children alongside the Literacy Subscale. This did not surprise us because the Diversity Subscale measures the sensitivity of educators to cater for the individual and group needs of children. It is the Subscale that picks up on differentiation of pedagogy and content to support children with additional needs (e.g., English as an Second Language children or children with special needs) and those with diverse backgrounds to ensure successful and meaningful learning for all.

The Planning for and Supporting Individual Learning Needs Item has had the most changes. During the writing of this scale, we are in the continuing throes of the COVID-19 pandemic, and many more children, for years to come, might be affected by this. There is compelling evidence that shows, during the pandemic, especially for disadvantaged and vulnerable children, there has been: (1) loss of time in formal and informal child care (a bigger percentage of their lives than for older children); (2) poorer quality home learning environments; (3) increased exposure to risks at home; (4) worsening parent mental health; (5) poorer access to play space; (6) lower physical activity; and (7) loss of access to a range of vital services (including severely reduced health visitor access) (Education Endowment Foundation, 2020–2022; Pascal et al., 2020). Other issues include the global economic crisis and the impact of a growing number of children living in vulnerable households.

Our revised Item on Planning for and Supporting Individual Learning Needs, therefore, required a sharper focus on the planning documents and record keeping for each child and for groups of children. We have added a bigger focus on disability and special and particular needs, for instance, drawing attention to those with disabilities in a positive way and planning for a diverse range of abilities. In particular, we have strengthened the exemplification material with each Item to support and provide concrete examples for researchers and educators. There is also a more apparent focus on inclusion across the three Items in this Subscale. During our training experience in countries like Canada, New Zealand, and Australia, we saw the need to separate out and emphasize inclusivity and focus on Indigenous peoples and not just those who are part of a multicultural society. In the Race Equality and Awareness Item we make specific reference to Indigenous groups so that countries experiencing this phenomenon can rate the inclusivity of all their cultural and racial heritage. One Indicator is nonapplicable to countries without Indigenous populations.

The Gender Equality and Awareness Item has also been modified to reflect more inclusivity of more diverse families. All three Items, therefore, have been modified and offer better and more exemplars in the additional notes to help observers know what to look for, what to ask, and what to note during assessment of this Subscale.

Reliability and Validity

The earlier version of this scale, called the Early Childhood Environment Rating Scale—Extension (ECERS-E; Sylva et al., 2003/2011), was shown to have good interobserver agreement and both concurrent and predictive validity. Because the ECQRS-EC includes four new items and earlier items have been updated and supplemented with more contemporary examples, we welcome new studies of reliability and validity.

Reliability. Good interobserver reliability on the ECERS-E is reported in Sylva et al. (1999, 2006).

Concurrent Validity. The total ECERS-E scores correlated (Sylva et al., 1999) with the Gold Standard instrument at the time, the ECERS-R (Harms et al., 2004).

Predictive Validity. Total scores and some Subscales from the ECERS-E predicted the academic and social development of more than 2,800 children in the EPPSE study between the ages of 3 and 5 (Sylva et al., 2006) and also between ages 5 and 11 years (Sylva et al., 2008). A newer longitudinal study on quality in early childhood centers (Melhuish & Gardner, 2023) also showed the positive effects of the ECERS-E on the developmental progress of a large English sample of children between ages 2 and 5. In Germany, Anders et al. (2012) demonstrated the positive effects of the ECERS-E on children's progress in mathematics.

Scoring the ECQRS-EC Using the Items From the ECERS-E. Researchers who wish to score the new ECQRS-EC in the same way as used in the validation studies cited above should remove the new items (Items 7, 10, 11c, 14) before analysis.

Content of the ECQRS-EC Scales

The ECQRS-EC covers four areas of practice: Literacy, Mathematics, Science, and Diversity and Inclusion. These broad domains are referred to as SUBSCALES. Each subheading within a SUBSCALE is referred to as an ITEM, and each text block within the ITEM is referred to as an INDICATOR. For example (see also page 24):

SUBSCALE = Language and Emergent Literacy
ITEM = Environmental Print: Letters and Words
INDICATOR 1.1 = No labeled pictures are visible to the children.

The Subscales and Items are as follows:

Preparing to Use the ECQRS-EC

If the ECQRS-EC is being used for research purposes, it is strongly recommended that you attend appropriate training, which is available from the authors. If the scale is being used for professional or practice development, it is also strongly recommended that the user undertakes appropriate training or is familiar with the use of rating scales. For a comprehensive assessment of quality in your center, the ECQRS-EC can be used alongside the other scales in the CLIQRS family of products: SSTEW (Siraj et al., 2015, 2024), MOVERS (Archer & Siraj, 2017, 2024), and PLEY (Siraj & Kingston, in press). Readers may also be familiar with the Environment Rating Scales: Early Childhood Environment Rating Scale—3 (ECERS-3; Harms et al., 2014, or ECERS-4, forthcoming), Infant/Toddler Environment Rating Scale—3 (ITERS-3; Harms et al., 2017), School-Age Care Environment Rating Scale—Revised (SACERS-R; Harms et al., 2015), and Family Child Care Environment Rating Scale—3 (FCCERS-3; Harms et al., 2019).

Using the ECQRS-EC demands a high level of understanding, not only about the content of the scale but also in terms of making sense of what is being observed. In addition to the content of the scale, you will need to understand the paperwork/files found in the center, including any planning and learning journals that are typically kept to support a child's learning and for assessment purposes.

You may need to ask nonleading questions of the staff to supplement your understanding. You will therefore need to feel confident in your interviewing skills and be able to respectfully, nonjudgmentally, and sensitively question educators to access important information. For these reasons we suggest that it is important for assessors using any of the CLIQRS scales to have a good grounding in early years practice, cultural sensitivity, and child development.

Before embarking on your first formal assessment, it is strongly recommended that the user conducts several trial observations to familiarize themself with the content of the items included in the scale. This can be done alone but is more beneficial if done with someone more familiar with the scales or with a "critical friend."

Finally, before making an observation, it is essential that you have, ready at hand, all of the paperwork/files and other materials needed to complete the task.

Timing

Typically, the observation should be completed during one session of 3–4 hours in the morning or afternoon. Observe only one group of children at a time. All areas to which children have access, both indoors and outside, should be observed. If you intend to observe other groups, then additional sessions will be needed. Additional time will be required if you need to consult planning records or talk to a member of staff for evidence to support a judgment. This should be done without other distractions.

If you are conducting observations on several scales, such as conducting the SSTEW scale along with the ECQRS-EC, then you will need to set aside a whole day and allow sufficient time to make comprehensive assessments, especially those that focus on interactions between adults/children and children/children. Plan your time carefully and overestimate rather than underestimate the time you will need to make a reasoned judgment of an activity/interaction.

Contextual Information on the Center

The instrument is designed to be used on a typical day with one group (class) of children in the age range between 3 and 6 years (i.e., after age 3 but before age 6). The user should have access to all areas (indoors and outside) that the children/adults are in.

Before the observation, gather background information about the center: its layout; names, numbers, and designations of the educators; and any planning for the session, including what activities will be available and the typicality of the day. It is helpful to complete the informational paperwork, such as the number of children in the groups, age range, and so forth, ahead of the observation.

Definitions

Note that throughout the scale, the word "educator" (or staff) is used as a generic term to cover the range of adults who work regularly with children in the center being observed. This could include volunteers and/or trainees/students as well as paid adults. Do not include adults who do not work on a regular basis with the children.

There are various quantitative terms used in the Indicators, and it is important that you are clear about the meaning of these. Before commencing an inter-rater reliability observation, check that all parties understand and can apply these terms accurately and consistently.

The following definitions apply:

Few = 2 or 3 (when quantifying objects)
Some = 4 or 5 (when quantifying objects)
Many = more than 5 (when quantifying objects)
Sometimes = at least 2 or 3 times, but less than the majority of times

Majority/most = 50% or more

Often = more than twice for interactions and every 1–2 weeks approximately, or more frequently, for planned activities.

For example, for Subscale 1: Language and Emergent Literacy, Item 1: Environmental Print: Letters and Words, Indicator 3.1 uses the term "a few." This suggests a limited number; the Notes for Clarification explain "few" as 2 or 3. Then in Indicator 5.1, the term "many" is used, which is clarified as more than 5.

Some Items require you to make a judgment about "most children" based upon what you see. For example, for Subscale 3: Emergent Science, Item 15c: Science Activities: Food Preparation, Indicator 5.2, "most children" would typically suggest more than 50 percent, and this may be evidenced by planning documents. However, if you notice that children appear to be consistently excluded from some activities and practices, you should not give credit for that Indicator.

There are Indicators that do not always follow the rules above, so it is important to read carefully, before starting an observation, all the Notes for Clarification, which provide supplemental information and examples. For example, for Subscale 1: Language and Emergent Literacy, Item 4: Sounds in Words, Indicator 7.2 says, "Some attention is given to linking sounds to letters.*" This is clarified in the Notes for Clarification as follows: "To give credit, observers should either see *two* examples of adults linking sounds to letters or see *one* example and find two examples in the sample of planning reviewed. Examples might include phonics work that makes the link between letters and sounds explicit, or an adult helping a child to write down a particular spoken word."

Where resources are described as "accessible" it means that children can get to them unassisted and for a substantial part of the day (more than half). It should be noted that not all children will have access to these materials at all times. For example, for Subscale 1: Language and Emergent Literacy, Item 2: Book and Literacy Areas, Indicators 3.1, 3.2, and 5.1 use the terms "easily accessible" and "accessible" as it pertains to books. This means that children can reach and use materials easily, not necessarily that every child must be able to have access to all of them at all times.

Optional Scoring Systems

The first three Items for Subscale 2: Emergent Mathematics are always scored. The observer should then select either Shape; Sorting, Matching, and Comparing; or Subitizing for Mathematical Activities (Items 11a, 11b, or 11c). The first three Items for Subscale 3: Emergent Science are always scored. The observer should then select either Nonliving, Living Processes, or Food Preparation for Science Activities (Items 15a, 15b, or 15c).

As ECQRS-EC focuses on the provision for learning experiences, there may be activities not evident that nevertheless cover important aspects of curriculum provision. Before choosing optional items, look carefully at the activities on offer to select the Item on which you have the most evidence for scoring. If in doubt, you can score ***ALL*** Items, including the optional ones, and make a judgment on which optional Items most accurately reflect children's overall experiences in that curriculum area.

The idea behind the optional system is to make the observation manageable. The ECQRS-EC assesses complex pedagogical interactions, and it would be impossible (or unrealistic) to expect to see all the behaviors and activities listed during an observation. The optional Item system allows credit to be given for what is most evident on the observed day.

For example, the three optional science Items assess the same concepts (e.g., staff are encouraging children to use their senses to explore and talk about their experiences) during different activities. What to score can be decided on the day, but it would be good practice to score all optional Items and enter the highest scoring one. For example, if you see a baking activity, you might have gathered the most evidence for Food Preparation. In this case, you would complete the scoring for this Item and cross out the other two optional science Items. In this way, you can give the center credit for their best practice on the day.

In terms of scoring, always submit four Item scores for Emergent Science—Items 12, 13, 14, plus one of 15 (a, b, c)—and four Item scores for Emergent Mathematics—Items 8, 9, 10, plus one of 11 (a, b c). If educators are using the scales in a more developmental way (e.g., over time to support improvements in practice), then they might choose to use all of the optional Items.

Conducting the Observation

1. The Items do not have to be completed in the order in which they appear in the book. If a cooking activity is taking place, you may decide to score it immediately and then come back to other Items later. Some Items may be scored more easily than others.
2. Only score an Item after you have allowed sufficient time to make a reasoned judgment. This is particularly important for Items that demand observing the interactions between educator/child or child/child. You need to be sure that what you are observing is representative of the practices as a whole.
3. Take care not to interrupt the activities being observed. The observer should be like a "fly on the wall" and should avoid interacting unnecessarily with the children or educators. It is important to be as unobtrusive as possible and to remain neutral in your actions, expressions, and replies to questions. It might be worth deciding what you will say to inquisitive children in advance so as not to upset them or engage them for too long. Remain as neutral and inconspicuous as possible.
4. Make sure the scoring is both legible and sufficient to be easily photocopied, photographed, or scanned. It is recommended that you use a pencil and have an eraser with you to amend scoring as you work.
5. If you are unsure about something, make detailed notes on your score sheet and ensure they are clear enough for you to follow when you come back to them at the end of the observation to discuss them with a critical friend in order to make a sound judgment. This is particularly important if you are using the scales for self-evaluation and plan to give feedback to others on your observations.
6. A new score sheet should be used for each observation. You have permission to photocopy the summary score sheets *only* (found at the end of the booklet). All photocopying should be for your personal use only, and all assessors should have their own original ECQRS-EC.
7. Scoring, as it relates to positive practice, might depend on whether the educator(s) is accessible to all children on a regular basis. You need to be sure that what you are observing is representative of practice as a whole.
8. There are a few Indicators, typically at level 7, that make clear the different expectations for children of different age groups. The Notes for Clarification will make clear when an Indicator may not be appropriate when making observations of children who are not in the age range appropriate for this level of development. The latter have been marked with an N/A next to them.
9. Before you leave the center, make sure that you have scored all Items. It is difficult to score Items once you have left.
10. Remember to express your gratitude to all the adults you have encountered during the course of the observation.

Scoring the Scales

Scoring should only be completed once the observer is familiar with the scale. Read Items carefully, as it is essential that judgments are made exactly in accordance with the instructions given. Scores must reflect the observed practice and not some future plan the staff may have told you about.

1. The scale measures from 1 to 7 with: 1 = Inadequate, 3 = Minimal, 5 = Good, and 7 = Excellent.
2. The observer should always start with 1 and work through the rest of the scale systematically.
3. A rating of 1 must be given if **any** Indicator in section 1 is scored YES.
4. A rating of 2 is given when **all** Indicators under 1 are scored NO and at least half of the Indicators under 3 are scored YES.
5. A rating of 3 is given when **all** Indicators under 1 are scored NO and **all** Indicators under 3 are scored YES.
6. A rating of 4 is given when **all** Indicators under 3 are met and at least half of the Indicators under 5 are scored YES.
7. A rating of 5 is given when **all** Indicators under 5 are scored YES.
8. A rating of 6 is given when **all** Indicators under 5 are met and at least half of the Indicators under 7 are scored YES.
9. A rating of 7 is given when **all** Indicators under 7 are scored YES.
10. A score of N/A (Not Applicable) may only be given for entire Items where there are options (e.g., 11a, Shape; 11b, Sorting, Matching, and Comparing; or 11c, Subitizing. These Items have an N/A option on the score sheet.
11. There are a few Indicators within Items, typically at level 7, that may not be appropriate when observing younger children. For example, in Item 14, unless there are children aged 4½ to 6 in the group, these Indicators should be N/A (Not Applicable). If the observed group consists of only children under 4½ and there is not an appropriately adapted version of the Indicator, you should mark these items N/A and note your reasons for this on the score sheet.
12. To calculate average Subscale scores, add up the scores for each Item in the Subscale and divide by the number of Items scored. The total mean scale score is the sum of all Item scores for the entire scale, divided by the number of Items scored.
13. Some users of the scale do not score the 3s, 5s, or 7s on an Item that was scored 1. However, researchers and other users continue to score all Indicators in an Item despite a score of 1 because they want a fuller picture of quality.

ECQRS-EC and the "Spirit of the Scales"

Although the individual Subscales bear the titles of curriculum areas such as Emergent Mathematics, the quality ratings within each Item are tuned to pedagogy and resources as well as to curriculum. Across the four Subscales, each Item is scored with reference to pedagogy, resources, and the center's organization. Individual Indicators usually focus on one of these at a time.

Centers that score well on the ECQRS-EC will be those in which there is a balance of child- and adult-initiated activity and a good deal of "sustained shared thinking" based on intentional pedagogy of co-construction (Siraj et al., 2023; Siraj-Blatchford et al., 2002). Credit is also given across all four Subscales based on evidence of planning and child assessment according to children's individual needs and interests.

Cautions in Use

The original ECERS-E was primarily developed as a tool for research, but it had become increasingly used to guide practice. The ECQRS-EC builds on the ECERS-E, but with a stronger focus on the emerging curriculum and professional development. This is very much in keeping with the principles of the CLIQRS.

It should, however, be kept in mind that a rating scale is not a simplistic checklist. The ECQRS-EC focuses on certain aspects of curricular provision (e.g., literacy, math, etc.) while not addressing others (e.g., personal, social, and emotional development; information technology; etc.). The fact that these other aspects of provision are not addressed by the ECQRS-EC does not mean that they are less important than literacy, math, and science, but simply that these emergent skills often form the basis of school learning that will follow. When used alongside other observational scales, ECQRS-EC adds greater depth by focusing on the emerging curriculum and provides educators with further guidance on pedagogical approaches that research has shown lead to beneficial outcomes for overall holistic child development.

The ECQRS-EC, having been developed from what was primarily a research tool, does not provide a comprehensive series of steps to work through in developing quality within a particular area. Rather, it contains a series of Indicators of quality at each level. For example, the Indicators representing a rating of 7 (Excellent) within the Item Emergent Writing/Mark Making are examples of the kinds of provision one might see in excellent centers. However, they do not necessarily include every single requirement one would expect in a high-quality environment. It's useful to think of Items and total scores in the ECQRS-EC as litmus tests; they suggest the presence of quality at a particular level, but they do not assess the full list of activities, interactions, and resources that comprise the ***TOTAL QUALITY*** of a center. Thus, a score on an Item or even the total score *estimates* the true or the full quality, but it *records* only a fraction of what makes a difference in children's lives.

It is important that centers do not adopt a checklist approach and address only the requirements listed in the ECQRS-EC to the exclusion of other improvements simply because they are the ones that are listed. This would not be in the spirit of the scales.

As stated above, the ECQRS-EC cannot cover all aspects of preschool practice, nor does it provide universal coverage within Subscales. Centers that score at 7 (Excellent) across the board will still need to consider their developmental needs—there is always room for improvement.

Using ECQRS-EC as a Self-Assessment and Improvement Tool

Centers that have been successful in using the CLIQRS and other observational rating scales for critically evaluating their own provision and practices have found them particularly useful as tools to open a debate among their workforce or center staff about what constitutes "quality." Having this debate before embarking on the administration of the scales can lead to a more supportive culture in which to make changes and a deeper understanding of quality. During training sessions, educators have often commented on how they value "working with the scales" as opposed to having ECQRS-EC, or any other rating scale, "done to them."

Making Judgments

Scores should provide the educators with an overall and professional judgment of how well the center is doing in helping children to develop some fundamental academic skills, nurtured in an environment that respects children's individual needs, backgrounds, gender, and heritage.

Observers should be mindful of the following when deciding on a score:

Inadequate (1): The environment at this level is not conducive to the adults actively engaging with children in a meaningful way. The practice observed is unlikely to support the academic development of children and in addition could harm children's developing positive self-image, self-worth, and self-concept and damage their view of themselves as active, autonomous, and engaged learners and thinkers.

Minimal (3): The practice provides a respectful, positive environment in which the children are expected to play and learn by themselves with educators facilitating but not necessarily supporting and extending learning experiences. Educators are attentive to children. They communicate in a pleasant manner. There are incidents of considered practice, but these appear to be coincidental, with little intentional pedagogy. While some academic concepts may be introduced, they may not always be age appropriate or presented in a developmentally appropriate manner. Educators do not always show consistent approaches to children, and their knowledge of child development appears superficial; this can be more evident when there are children of mixed ages in a room.

Good (5): The practice supports engagement with the children and encourages autonomy. It recognizes children's interests and individual needs, but may miss some opportunities to extend thinking and scaffold learning. Educators can respond to both child-initiated and planned activities in a way that supports and extends children's learning. The educators assess, plan, and support children in exploring the world around them through a range of academic subjects.

Excellent (7): Relational and intentional pedagogies are clearly evident. Practice scaffolds learning through encouragement and modeling. Practice at this level shows intentional pedagogy with the staff using their knowledge, judgments, and expertise to organize learning experiences that are engaging for all children. Learning experiences support curiosity and problem-solving. Staff pedagogy includes planning for and building on individual children's interests to encourage growth in language, thinking, and learning.

Moving from Inadequate toward Excellent also involves increasing knowledge, thought, and implementation by the educator to improve both the indoor and the outdoor environments for learning. Pedagogy moves from more intuitive responses that may happen by chance or be inconsistent, toward an increasingly intentional pedagogy. This may include giving feedback, assessing, and planning for an individual child/group, deeply engaging with and extending children's development and learning.

Gaining an accurate overall picture of practice and provision requires a considered response to all Indicators, and these will necessarily vary according to the behaviors, responses, and interactions under scrutiny. They may be positive and likely to enhance the children's learning and development, neutral and adding little to children's learning, or negative and potentially harmful.

Example of Positive Practice:

Subscale 1: Language and Emergent Literacy
Item 6: Talking and Listening
Indicator 7.1: Adults provide scaffolding for children's conversations with them.*
Indicator 7.2: Children are often encouraged to talk to each other in small groups, and adults encourage their peers to listen to them.* P
Indicator 7.3: Adults regularly extend children's language through encouraging complex sentences that require children to consider the future or the imagined world (e.g., "What do you think might happen if . . . ?" or "What might happen next?").*
Indicator 7.4: Children are encouraged to ask questions.*

In order to record a "yes" for these descriptions, we would expect the interaction to be observed more than once during the observation period because this is at the Excellent level. In addition, there would be an expectation, when making a judgment, that there is potential for this practice to be experienced by all of the children in the center on a regular basis: that is, to ascertain that such experiences could happen daily and potentially with all children. It might be helpful to note which educators were observed engaging in the interactions so that it would be possible to identify who had those skills. If the skills are limited to one or two individuals in a large staff group, it would then be necessary to determine whether these educators have access to all of the children being observed and whether they would be available every day.

The judgments recognize the fact that some educators may be better at supporting children's learning and development than others, but judgments should consider a child's overall exposure to these types of experiences during their time in the center. Like many other similar scales, the center could potentially achieve high scores even though not all educators are able to support the children in the same way.

The same approach holds for the lower end of this item:

Example of Potentially Negative Practice:
Subscale 1: Language and Emergent Literacy
Item 6: Talking and Listening
Indicator 1.1: Very little encouragement or opportunity for children to talk to adults.
Indicator 1.2: Most verbal attention from adults is of a supervisory nature.*

The observer should look at the dominant behavior of the educator(s) during the period of the observation. While there may be some encouragement given to children, it is not seen consistently. Talk that is supervisory in nature will be the dominant mode, with the educator mostly remarking on the management of routines or behaviors or not even speaking to children. While there may be exceptions to this by some adults, it is sufficient to record a "yes" if, for example, in the outdoor area the supervising adults are huddled in a corner, chatting together for an extended period, rather than interacting with children. This would be consistent with judgments in other similar scales.

Where an asterisk (*) appears beside some indicators, this means that there are Notes for Clarification to refer to. These notes appear on the page following the list of Indicators. **It is essential that you read the Notes for Clarification,** as this will help you to further understand the Indicator. Please read each Indicator carefully, including all the Notes for Clarification, *before* using the ECQRS-EC.

Use of Supplementary (Nonobservation) Evidence

Since the ECQRS-EC began life as an observational research instrument (the ECERS-E), many Items can be given credit from directly observing the environment in which the children are learning. A score can be decided after a relatively short period of time. What sets the CLIQRS apart from other rating scales is its emphasis on behaviors and intentions, most specifically those of the educator(s) in the room.

The ECQRS-EC seeks to investigate the provision for emerging skills and understanding in academic subjects. The emphasis is not so much on what the educator has at their disposal (resources) to advance learning but on how they use resources to provide developmentally appropriate learning experiences for children. The emphasis here is on the pedagogy the educator uses to support learning within an emergent curriculum. Observing the pedagogy of an educator in a specific curriculum area demands the observer to be familiar with both pedagogy and subject-specific knowledge as applied to young children.

To give credit for some Items in the ECQRS-EC, the observer would have to observe practice over a substantial period of time for the score to be valid. The danger with some Items is that in a half-day visit, the observer may not be exposed to some of the curriculum areas covered by the scale. Subjects such as science may not be offered daily, so how could credit be given, or a judgment secured, for activities that may be part of the weekly plan but were not taking place at the time of the visit? In order to overcome this, the CLIQRS allows the use of supplementary evidence. This can be in the form of planning notes/journals/forecasts, room displays, or children's records/portfolios. Observers may also want to talk to the educators about their plans and intentions, and time to do this should be set aside at the end of the observation.

The asterisk (*) that appears beside some Items and/or Indicators in the pages that follow means that Notes for Clarification are provided to help the observer better understand the Item or Indicator and make informed judgments. The asterisk will be at the end of the Item and/or Indicator, and associated Notes for Clarification will appear on the following page. **It is essential that you read the Notes for Clarification** associated with these asterisks. It is **strongly** advised that you read through **all** the Notes for Clarification given for an Item or Indicator *before* starting an observation. Arriving at an accurate score depends on the observer being familiar with, and confident in applying, their understanding of Notes for Clarification when making a judgment.

Where it is appropriate to supplement observation with evidence from other sources, individual Indicators are annotated as follows:

P = evidence from planning is acceptable
D = evidence from displays/photographic records is acceptable
R = evidence from children's records is acceptable (includes children's portfolios or folders of completed work)
Q = evidence from questioning the educator is acceptable

It should be noted that these codes are also marked on the score sheet next to the relevant Indicators. When scoring, the letters can be circled to show which source of evidence has been used.

Throughout the scale, Indicators for which evidence other than observations can be used are marked accordingly (using P, D, R, and/or Q). A small number of these relate specifically to planning and/or records and *require* evidence to be present in these forms. For example, the following Indicator from Subscale 3: Emergent Science, Item 15a: Science Activities: Nonliving, requires planning for the introduction of scientific concepts. In this case, planning evidence is *required*:

> Indicator 5.1: Staff often plan and introduce appropriate scientific concepts (e.g., how materials change, magnetism, sinkers and floaters), and children handle materials.* P, D, R

However, for most of the items that allow evidence from supplementary sources, these additional sources of evidence should be sought only when observable examples are lacking. Observation always provides the best evidence, because there is no way of knowing how well a particular activity was carried out when using evidence from display or records (or, in the case of planning evidence, whether in fact the activity was carried out at all). For example, in the following Indicator from Subscale 3: Emergent Science, Item 12: Natural Materials, credit can be given if the activity is observed on the day. If no examples are directly observed, evidence from planning and/or display can be used:

> Indicator 5.1: Natural materials are used beyond decoration to illustrate specific concepts (e.g., planting seeds or bulbs to illustrate growth, seed dispersal).* P, D

Do not give credit for activities shown in the planning when your observations on the day do not support the planning evidence. In some cases, evidence from planning, records, display, and/or questioning can be used only as *supporting* evidence, and a particular activity must also be observed to give credit. **In these cases, the P, D, R, and Q are shown in parentheses.** For example:

Subscale 3: Emergent Science
Item 12: Natural Materials
Indicator 7.1: Children are encouraged to identify and explore a range of natural phenomena in their environment outside the center and talk about/describe them.* (P), (D)

The Notes for Clarification for this Indicator make it clear that at least one discussion relating to nature/natural materials should be observed. Planning or display evidence can then be used as *supporting evidence* that children experience a range of natural phenomena.

In order to make a sound judgment about the intentionality of an educator's practice, it may be necessary to ask questions about what you have observed, especially if this has involved an interaction with an individual child or group. It is important that the educator knows beforehand that you might want to ask some questions to help you with your observations. Questioning an educator should be done sensitively. Consider the following as starting points for digging deeper into the intentions of the educator without appearing judgmental:

Tell me a little bit more about . . . .
I wasn't sure about . . . .
How do you decide what to put out for . . . ?
What do you normally do if . . . .
How do you monitor . . . .
How are children chosen for . . . .
How do you support . . . .
How do you manage . . . .
Your work with . . . . Tell me a bit more about what was going on.
Why did you choose that equipment?

The Score Sheet, Joint Observation Sheet, and ECQRS-EC Profile

A separate Score Sheet is available for you to photocopy at the end of the book (beginning after page 76). It makes the recording of scores much easier if you can view the Item/Indicators and the Score Sheet together.

The Joint Observation/Inter-rater Reliability score sheet (page 83) is designed to support discussion between different assessors and to illustrate a final agreed score. When observations are undertaken by more than one assessor in the same center, such as during training and/or to ensure inter-rater reliability, typically the observers will set aside a time at the end of their observations to discuss their scores. The agreed score may be an average of the observers' original scores, but more typically one observer has seen some practice that is important and has been missed by the other observer(s). All of the observers must give evidence to support their scores, and a final score is agreed upon after discussion (which may be the original score of one observer).

The ECQRS-EC Profile (page 84) allows you to plot *three* sets of observations. This can be useful to highlight differences between assessors and/or to show progress over time. If you plot the scores using different-colored ink (or in some other way indicate differences), you should potentially see progress over time (if the observations are conducted at different times) or be able to track differences between assessors.

Content of the Scales

The scales include four areas of practice linked to particular aspects of development, called ***Subscales***. Within the Subscales there are 18 subsections called ***Items***.

Each Item has a number of blocks of text that describe practice, and these are called ***Indicators***.

The Subscales and Items are as follows:

Inadequate 1	2	Minimal 3	4	Good 5	6	Excellent 7

SUBSCALE 1: LANGUAGE AND EMERGENT LITERACY

Item 1: Environmental Print: Letters and Words

1.1 No labeled pictures are visible to the children.* D

1.2 No environmental print that is relevant to children on display.* D

3.1 A few labeled pictures are present and visible to children.* D

3.2 A few labeled objects or items are present and easily visible to the children (e.g., labels on shelves, children's names on coat pegs or paintings, pots labeled "pens" or "pencils").*

3.3 Printed words are prominently displayed (e.g., "welcome" on the door, titles on art displays, labels designating interest centers within the room such as the art area or sand/water area).* D

5.1 Many labeled pictures are on view to the children, indicating a print-rich environment.* D

5.2 Children are encouraged to recognize printed words in their environment (e.g., their own names on peg labels, print on everyday objects such as food packaging or shopping bags).*

5.3 Children are encouraged to recognize letters in their environment (e.g., staff draw attention to the individual letters in a child's name or in other environmental print).*

7.1 Discussion of environmental print takes place and often relates to objects of personal interest to the children.*

7.2 There is discussion of the relationship between the spoken and the printed word (e.g., discussing how to read the words written on a child's T-shirt).*

7.3 Children are encouraged to recognize letters *and* words in their environment other than their own names (e.g., in words on labels or posters).*

(See Notes for Clarification on next page and see page 20 for an explanation of the use of letter codes and parentheses for observations.)

Notes for Clarification

1.1, 3.1, 5.1 For "labeled pictures," do not count print without pictures. Pictures must be accompanied by brief text relating to the content of the picture (e.g., a poster of a car with the word "car" printed below, drawer labels with pictures and text labels to identify the contents). The text must be in large enough print to be read from a distance and to be read by the children.

1.2 Environmental print includes all printed words in the child's environment, including words that are attached to or superimposed on an object that has meaning to the child. To be truly "environmental" it must have meaning relevant to the object it relates to, for example, storage signs that include a picture and the name of the stored items, labels on shelves/children's pegs, print on packaging/clothing/shopping bags, printed instructions on picture signs ("Please wash your hands"). These can be handwritten as well as printed. Words that form part of resources (e.g., books, games, flashcards) are not considered to be environmental print as they have no illustrative meaning attached to the words. Do not count displays or other text that are relevant to adults rather than to children.

3.1, 3.2 Few = Two or three different examples.

3.3 Print may be above eye level, but children should be able to see it easily.

5.1 To give credit, at least five (many) or more different examples should be present and easily visible to the children. The observer should be satisfied that the environment is print-rich in order to give credit.

5.2 To give credit, staff should be observed explicitly encouraging children to recognize environmental print (at least one example observed) or the observer should see evidence of a regular daily routine that encourages children to recognize print in the environment (e.g., a self-registration system where children find their names and post them on a board to show that they are present).

5.3 At least one example of adults drawing explicit attention to letters should be observed.

7.1 Discussions must actively involve children and be more extensive than a passing mention. At least two examples must be observed, one of which must relate to an item clearly of personal interest to the children (e.g., a child's T-shirt, print on postcards sent by other children in the group, print on an object a child has brought in from home).

7.2 Discussion must actively involve children. At least one example should be observed.

7.3 To give credit, observers should see at least one example of staff encouraging children to recognize words in the environment, and at least one example of staff encouraging children to recognize letters.

Inadequate		Minimal		Good		Excellent
1	2	3	4	5	6	7

Item 2: Book and Literacy Areas

Inadequate (1)	Minimal (3)	Good (5)	Excellent (7)
1.1 Books are unattractive.*	3.1 Some books of different kinds are accessible to children.*	5.1 A variety of types of book is accessible to children.*	7.1 Book area is comfortable (rug and cushions or comfortable seating) and filled with a wide range of books of varied style, content, and complexity.*
1.2 Books are not of a suitable age level.*	3.2 An easily accessible area of the room is set aside for books.*	5.2 Book area used independently by children.*	7.2 Adults encourage children to use books and direct them to the book area.*
	3.3 Some reading takes place in the book area.*		7.3 Books are included in learning areas outside of the book corner.*

(See Notes for Clarification on next page and see page 20 for an explanation of the use of letter codes and parentheses for observations.)

Notes for Clarification

1.1 This refers to the books themselves and not the way in which they are displayed. Score yes if 50% or more of the books are damaged.

1.2 Score yes if 50% or more of the books are of an unsuitable age level.

3.1 "Some" means four or five. Different kinds include picture/story books, reference/information books, poetry/nursery rhymes, and counting/math books. Not all categories are required, but at least three or four examples from two different categories should be accessible to children daily.

3.2 The book area may also be used for other quiet activities and/or for whole group time at certain times of the day but must generally be intended for the purposeful reading of books.

3.3 This could be during whole group time or informally, by groups or individual children, with or without adults. This indicator is specifically concerned with how extensively the book area (or areas) is used. Do not give credit if books are taken from the book area and used elsewhere (e.g., children select books from the book corner to read at the table while waiting for snack).

5.1 See Indicator 3.1 for possible categories of books. Books could be commercially produced or homemade. At least three examples from each category should be accessible to children daily (and observers should also base their decision on the size of the group being catered for). In addition, the selection should include many books with text, and some variation in the level of books available to cater for different skills (e.g., some simpler and some more complex, dual language texts or books in other languages where the group is diverse).

5.2 At least two (different) examples must be observed. However, observers should also base their judgment on the size of the group when determining whether children regularly access the book area independently of adults. Children must be accessing the book area for the purpose of selecting and reading books rather than for any other activity.

7.1 In addition to the variety of types required for Indicator 5.1, this Indicator requires variety *within* the types of books offered to cater for a range of interests (e.g., information books about science topics, transport topics, and different cultures/religions; story books about animals, people, and imaginary creatures). Sizes and formats should vary. A greater variation in developmental level is also required than is necessary for Indicator 5.1. The area should contain books at many different levels, ranging from simple board books and books with many pictures/little text, to more complex books with a lot of text on each page and other more complex features (e.g. reference books with diagrams).

7.2 This should be observed at least once.

7.3 Books should be provided in at least two other areas to give credit and should have some connection to the learning/play experiences provided in that area (e.g., counting books in the math area).

Inadequate 1	2	Minimal 3	4	Good 5	6	Excellent 7

Item 3: Adults Reading With the Children

1	3	5	7
1.1 Adults rarely read to the children.* P, Q	3.1 Adults read with children daily.* P, Q 3.2 There is some involvement of the children during reading times (e.g., children are encouraged to join in with repetitive words and phrases in the text, adult shares pictures with the children or asks simple questions).*	5.1 Children take an active role during reading times, and the words and/or story are usually discussed.* 5.2 Children are encouraged to use conjecture and/or link the content of the book to other experiences.*	7.1 There is discussion about print and letters as well as content.* 7.2 There is support material for the children to engage with stories by themselves (e.g., tapes, interactive displays, puppets, story sacks, computer games). D 7.3 There is evidence of one-to-one reading with some children.*

(See Notes for Clarification on next page and see page 20 for an explanation of the use of letter codes and parentheses for observations.)

Notes for Clarification

1.1 Score yes if no reading with the children is seen during the observation and there is no daily reading time listed on the schedule.

3.1 Give credit if two or more examples of informal reading with groups or individual children are seen during the observation. Alternatively, credit can be given if there is evidence of a planned daily reading time that includes all (or the majority of) the children even if this happens outside the observation time. This could be whole group reading or planned small group reading times.

3.2 Reading with children must be observed on at least one occasion in order to score this Indicator. If several reading times are observed, the involvement of children should be a feature of the majority of sessions in order to give credit.

5.1 This must be observed at least once. If several reading sessions are observed, this should be true for most sessions.

5.2 Examples might include an adult asking, "What do you think [the character] will do next?" or (when reading a factual book about pets) "Have any of you got a pet at home? How do you take care of them?" If several reading sessions are observed, this should be true for most sessions.

7.1 This should be observed at least once to give credit.

7.3 Some are four or five. Examples should be observed. It should be clear that informal reading with individual children is a regular part of the daily routine.

Inadequate 1	2	Minimal 3	4	Good 5	6	Excellent 7

Item 4: Sounds in Words*

1	3	5	7
1.1 Few or no rhymes or poems are spoken or sung.* P, Q	3.1 Rhymes are often spoken or sung by adults to children.* P, Q	5.1 The rhyming components of songs/rhymes are brought to the attention of children.*	7.1 Attention is paid to syllabification of words (e.g., through clapping games, jumping, etc.).* P
	3.2 Children are encouraged to speak and/or sing rhymes.*	5.2 The initial sounds in words are brought to the attention of children.*	7.2 Some attention is given to linking sounds to letters.* (P)

(See Notes for Clarification on next page and see page 20 for an explanation of the use of letter codes and parentheses for observations.)

Notes for Clarification

Rhymes could include nursery rhymes and other rhyming songs, poems, rhyming games played on the computer, card games that involve rhymes, rhyming books, or phonics activities that include rhyme. Give credit for rhymes spoken or sung with small groups of children, as well as whole group activities. If songs are used as evidence, credit can only be given if these are rhyming songs. Adults must be actively involved. For example, do not give credit if you see children listening to taped songs/rhymes by themselves.

1.1 Score yes if there is evidence that rhymes are spoken or sung fewer than two or three times per week (e.g., only one singing time scheduled per week and no evidence of informal singing during the session observed).

3.1 "Often" means daily. Give credit if there is evidence of a planned daily singing/rhyme session that includes all (or the majority of) the children, even if this occurs outside the observation period. Depending on the number of children attending, this may be carried out in a small group rather than as a whole class activity. If there is no daily group session planned, then at least two examples of informal use of rhyme (e.g., singing, rhyming books) with small groups or individual children should be seen during the observation.

3.2 It is not necessary for adults to draw explicit attention to rhyme to give credit at this level. For example, give credit if it is observed that children usually join in during singing sessions with rhymes or when reading a rhyming book.

5.1 At least one example must be observed.

5.2 At least two examples must be observed. Adults must draw explicit attention to the initial sounds in words and say the words out loud (e.g., drawing attention to the fact that "bat" and "ball" start with the same letter by saying, "Can you hear? They both begin with 'b.' Can you think of anything else that starts with the same sound?").

7.1 Give credit if this is seen during the observation. If no examples are observed on the day, then at least two examples should be found in the sample of planning reviewed.

7.2 To give credit, observers should either see *two* examples of adults linking sounds to letters or see *one* example and find two examples in the sample of planning reviewed. Examples might include phonics work that makes the link between letters and sounds explicit, or an adult helping a child to write down a particular spoken word.

Inadequate 1	2	Minimal 3	4	Good 5	6	Excellent 7

Item 5: Emergent Writing/Mark Making*

Inadequate (1)	Minimal (3)	Good (5)	Excellent (7)
1.1 There are no materials for children to engage in emergent writing.* 1.2 Children never observe staff writing down what they (the children) say.* D, R	3.1 Children have access to implements for writing (e.g., pencils, felt tip markers, chalk).* 3.2 Children have access to paper or other resources appropriate to a writing task (e.g., paper or telephone pads, chalk boards, small whiteboards for use with dry erase markers).* 3.3 Children sometimes observe staff writing down what they (the children) say.* D, R	5.1 A place in the center is set aside for emergent writing.* 5.2 Children often observe staff writing down what they (the children) say.* 5.3 Children are encouraged to "have a go" at "writing" to communicate with others (e.g., homemade books, written menus in the "café," annotating their own picture).	7.1 As well as pencils and paper, the mark making area has a theme to encourage children to "write" (e.g., an office).* 7.2 Adults draw to children's attention the purpose of writing (e.g., addressing an envelope, making a shopping list, writing a story).* D, R, (P) 7.3 Children's emergent writing is displayed for others to see.* D

(See Notes for Clarification on next page and see page 20 for an explanation of the use of letter codes and parentheses for observations.)

Notes for Clarification

"Emergent" or "developing" writing is young children's own attempts at translating oral language into a written form. In its earliest stages, it may appear as lines and squiggles, but if asked, the child can usually tell you what they have "written." As children become more proficient, evidence of letters or numbers begins to emerge from this seemingly random mark making. Children copying what an adult has written is not classed as emergent writing.

1.1 Score yes if children do not have access to writing materials for at least some portion of the day.

1.2, 3.3 Observers should check displays and children's records/portfolios for evidence of staff writing down children's words (i.e., "scribing" for children). Examples might include children's artwork displayed with their words written as a caption underneath. For Indicators 1.2 and 3.3, evidence from records and displays can be used. To score no for Indicator 1.2, one example should be observed. Score yes for 3.3 if two examples are observed.

3.1, 3.2 To give credit, at least one mark making option should be available for children to access freely for much of the day (i.e., not restricted to "writing activities"). Variety in materials/media is considered at Indicator 5.1, and credit can be given at this minimal level even if the range of options is limited.

5.1 This must be a designated area (or areas) with suitable materials and space to write—it is not enough for children to have access to writing materials that they then take to any available table. A wider variety of materials to encourage mark making should also be available at this level. The variety could include a writing area that has pens, pencils, crayons, pads, rulers, calendars, charts, and diaries.

5.2 Score yes if three examples are observed.

7.1 Examples might include writing connected to role play, such as a shop with shopping lists, price tags, a cash register, etc. or a post office with parcels to label and stamp. In these areas children contribute to environmental print (e.g., writing labels for their drawers or for displays).

7.2 If a purposeful writing activity is not seen on the day, observers should look for evidence that such activities have taken place (e.g., displayed materials). At least three examples of purposeful writing should be found in the display and records reviewed. Confirmatory evidence can be sought in the planning. However, since the observer will not know how well planning is (or has been) carried out, credit for this Indicator should not be given solely on the basis of planning evidence.

7.3 Do not give credit for writing that is copied/traced from an adult's handwriting.

Inadequate 1	2	Minimal 3	4	Good 5	6	Excellent 7

Item 6: Talking and Listening*

Inadequate	Minimal	Good	Excellent
1.1 Very little encouragement or opportunity for children to talk to adults. 1.2 Most verbal attention from adults is of a supervisory nature.*	3.1 Some conversation between adults and children occurs (e.g., adults talk to the children either individually or as a group about an ongoing activity, ask simple questions, respond to children's comments). 3.2 Children are allowed to talk among themselves with some limited adult intervention (e.g., adults ask closed questions).	5.1 Interesting experiences are planned by adults and drawn upon to encourage talk and the sharing of ideas.* (P) 5.2 Children are encouraged to engage in conversations rather than single utterance speech. For example, staff might ask questions that require more than "yes" or "no" answers.* 5.3 Adults regularly create one-to-one opportunities to talk with children by initiating conversations with individuals.*	7.1 Adults provide scaffolding for children's conversations with them.* 7.2 Children are often encouraged to talk to each other in small groups, and adults encourage their peers to listen to them.* P 7.3 Adults regularly extend children's language through encouraging complex sentences that require children to consider the future or the imagined world (e.g., "What do you think might happen if . . . ?" or "What might happen next?").* 7.4 Children are encouraged to ask questions.*

(See Notes for Clarification on next page and see page 20 for an explanation of the use of letter codes and parentheses for observations.)

Notes for Clarification

Item 6 focuses on strategies for getting children to engage in extended conversations, often called "**scaffolding.**" Item 7 focuses on strategies regarding new words and encouraging children to follow conventional patterns of speech, such as adding "ed" for past tense and "s" for plurals. Item 6 is about encouraging conversations and taking turns, while Item 7 is about new vocabulary or specific ways of speaking.

1.2 Score yes if the majority (more than half) of adults' talk is related to managing routines or behavior.

5.1 Assesses the extent to which adults *plan* for talk. Experiences must have an explicit focus on communication and the sharing of ideas. "Nonliteracy" activities (e.g., science experiments) can be counted if there is a planned and explicit focus on discussion. Examples of appropriate planning might include listing key words or questions for a particular activity, or "brainstorming" at the beginning of a topic to gather children's ideas. As with all Items, planning evidence should be used with caution and *at least one planned activity must be observed* to assess how effectively adults draw on the experience to encourage children's talk. If this is not the case, credit should not be given.

5.2 Give credit for questions/prompts that require more than "yes" or "no" answers, but which are not as challenging as those required for Indicator 7.3 (e.g., an adult might ask, "Which animals are you going to put in the barn?" or "What do you plan to wear to the party?"). No specific number of examples is required, but observers should hear enough evidence to be sure that encouraging conversations is a regular occurrence. This Indicator is similar to Indicator 5.3 in Item 7 but it does not focus *specifically* on the use of open questions. Item 6 focuses on adults encouraging more than "yes" or "no" replies, which may be accomplished by other techniques besides open questions. Examples include requests such as "Tell us about your trip to the beach" or "Explain how you keep your feet dry when walking through a puddle."

5.3 Three or more examples should be observed, and one-to-one conversations with individual children should take place in a variety of contexts (e.g., during routines, during adult-led activities, and during child-initiated free play). Conversations at this level should also be more extensive than is required for Indicator 3.1 and should involve a number of back-and-forth communications between the adult and child.

7.1 Scaffolding language provides a framework of support for children's talk. To give credit, adults should be observed encouraging and extending children's verbal contributions in conversation (e.g., a child says, "Look, the beans are growing," and the adult responds, "Yes, that's right, they're growing really tall. How can we go about measuring them?"). No specific number of examples is required, but observers should see enough evidence of scaffolding conversations that they are confident they are not giving credit for an unusual occurrence but for the creation of genuine conversations.

7.2 The emphasis here is on small groups—do not count whole group discussions/circle times. The communication should be more focused on the language itself and not simply talking while taking part in a play activity. Examples might include children telling peers about models they have made or recalling a trip outside the center. If planning is used as evidence, the observer should be satisfied that the talk is likely to be of good quality and that children are encouraged to listen to each other (i.e., evidence from other observations should support this conclusion).

7.3 No specific number of examples is required, but observers should hear enough evidence to be sure that adults are deliberately encouraging children to build on their earlier utterances so that they continue and extend the conversation.

7.4 At least one example of encouragement must be observed. In addition, where children do ask questions spontaneously, adults should respond in an encouraging and respectful way (e.g., give the child time to ask the question, and respond with interest to the question).

Inadequate		Minimal		Good		Excellent
1	2	3	4	5	6	7

Item 7: Words and Sentences*

1.1 Staff do not draw children's attention to specific words or their meanings.

1.2 Staff do not model a rich and diverse vocabulary and tend to speak to children only about routine things using simple language.

1.3 Staff do not ask children questions throughout the day.

1.4 Staff always ignore children's word errors ("two sheeps") or sentence errors ("I digged a hole").*

3.1 Staff point out and explain unusual or new words while reading with children.*

3.2 Staff often speak to children during daily routines such as snack or lunch time.*

3.3 Staff use some closed questions to encourage children to speak.*

3.4 Staff occasionally paraphrase children's errors in words or sentences by substituting the conventional form of a word or word ending in place of the error.*

5.1 Throughout the day (not only during reading time) staff point out new or unusual words. This is sometimes called "labeling" things or actions.*

5.2 Staff extend children's sentences by repeating what the child has said while adding new information to the child's sentence.*

5.3 Staff often use open-ended questions to encourage children to reply using more than single words.*

5.4 Staff often paraphrase children's errors (words or sentences) by repeating what the child has said while substituting the conventional form of a word or a word ending.

7.1 After explaining the meaning of a new word, staff encourage children to practice it themselves.*

7.2 Staff model complex sentences when speaking with children in *both* formal (e.g., story time) and informal contexts (while joining in children's play).*

7.3 Staff actively encourage children to engage in back-and-forth peer conversations on their own.*

7.4 When paraphrasing a child's utterance that contained errors, staff draw attention to the correct usage, through, for example, special voice effects that highlight the conventional form to draw the child's attention to it.*

(See Notes for Clarification on next page and see page 20 for an explanation of the use of letter codes and parentheses for observations.)

Notes for Clarification

Item 7 focuses on adult strategies with regard to new words and to encouraging children to follow conventional patterns of speech, such as adding "ed" for past tense and "s" for more than one. In contrast, Item 6 focuses on adult strategies for getting children to engage in extended conversations, often called "scaffolding." When children do not use conventional endings or forms of speech, credit in Item 7 is given for the adults modeling the conventional form while never implying that they disapprove of the child's use of nonconventional language. The adults convey to the child that there are several ways of speaking and the adult has modeled a different way.

1.4 Both are errors; the first is an error in forming the irregular plural of the noun sheep and the second an error in the irregular past tense for the verb dig. In both examples, the child has overgeneralized the normal rules for the endings of words. Overgeneralizations of this kind show that children have learned *rules* for words and sentences; the English language has many irregularities that children must master.

3.1 In pointing out a new word, adults speak slowly and clearly and/or use special voice effects to highlight the new word.

3.2 Speaking clearly helps children distinguish the individual sounds in words (e.g., "Today we are going to eat a fresh PINEAPPLE" [spoken with clear enunciation of individual letter sounds]).

3.3 A closed question requires only a one-word answer (e.g., "How old are you?", "What color did you paint the pig?").

3.4 An adult paraphrases a child's incorrect utterance (an error in a word or in a word ending) by substituting the correct form of the word in the place of the child's error. The adult may extend the sentence with additional words, but this is not necessary. What matters is that the adult has gently substituted a conventional form of language in place of the child's error. One example is sufficient.

5.1 To give credit, the new word must be introduced *outside* of story time. It may involve special voice effects such as special intonation to stress the importance or meaning of a word (e.g., "Your bucket was full and now it is EMPTY"). Other examples include using sound effects to draw attention to the meaning of a word (e.g., "The bees were BUZZING [sound effects] inside their hive").

5.2 "Extending" speech means repeating what the child said but adding something new so that the meaning of the sentence is extended. Extensions usually create a longer sentence than the child's original words. Child: "I ate cake at my birthday." Adult: "You ate cake at your birthday party, and friends from the nursery came to your house."

5.3 An open-ended question cannot be answered by a single-word answer but requires the child to answer using several words: "What did do for your birthday over the weekend?" "How will you put out the fire in the doll's house?" Open-ended questions often begin with How? or Why? However, note that "How many?" is a question requiring only a single-word answer. To gain credit, staff must be observed to use open questions in addition to closed ones, three or more times.

7.1 The encouragement to repeat a new word may be very gentle. For example, staff may say, "Beautiful [repeating the word they have just said themselves]. That's a hard word to say. Can you try saying it? I'll go first. Beautiful. Now it's your turn to say this word."

7.2 Complex sentences are usually five or more words long. Many complex sentences join two thoughts together. ("The girl escaped from the dragon *by* holding tight to the star.") Other complex sentences describe a sequence of actions. ("*Before* he put on his party costume, the little boy jumped up to the window.")

7.3 A back-and-forth conversation is one in which both partners take at least two turns, speaking on a single (shared) topic. To gain credit for this Indicator, the observer must witness staff encouraging a child to speak to another child about something specific. For example, staff might say, "Why don't you and Sarah ask the new girl [Evie] if she has any brothers or sisters?" or "Why don't you and Jaxon decide which one of you will be the first to ride the trike when we go outside today?"

7.4 Staff paraphrasing a child's speech error must make salient the conventional way to speak. "Yes, all the sheep were very hungry, all the *sheep* [stressed truncated word]." They do this by introducing another form of speech while not disapproving of what the child has said. Credit in Indicator 7.4 is given for introducing the child to options. Adults can explain to older children that "sheep" is a tricky word that does not take the "s" that is usually added to a word to specify more than one. They may also explain that many action words add "ed" to the end of the word to tell the listener that the action took place in the past. However, we do not follow this regular rule for the word "dig," and we say "dug" instead to specify that the action took place in the past. Such explanations are not appropriate for younger children, for whom informally demonstrating the conventional word is all that is appropriate.

Inadequate		Minimal		Good		Excellent
1	2	3	4	5	6	7

SUBSCALE 2: EMERGENT MATHEMATICS

NOTE: Items 8, 9, and 10 *MUST* be assessed. After assessing these Items, you may then select *EITHER* Item 11a, Item 11b, or Item 11c. Choose the Item that is most relevant to the content of the observation or the age of the children.

Item 8: Counting and the Application of Counting*

1.1 Children rarely take part in activities or routines where counting is used.* P, D, R, Q

1.2 Very few resources are available to encourage the children to take part in counting activities (e.g., seeds, shells, buttons, counting books, games).*

3.1 Number activities, counting books, games, songs, or rhymes are used with the children at least once a week.* P, D, R, Q

3.2 Numbers are named and observable at least once, as part of daily routines.

3.3 Math provision includes at least two different resources that encourage children to take part in counting activities daily (e.g., posters featuring numbers, sets of countable objects, counting books, games, or other resources). D

5.1 Number activities such as songs, rhymes, counting books, and/or games are used daily with the children.* (P), (D), (R)

5.2 Children are encouraged to count objects and to associate the spoken numbers with the numerical concepts (e.g., counting the number of children present at registration, counting out six milk cartons for six children, asking a child to count the number of blocks in a tower they have made).*

5.3 Adults use ordinal numbers (1st, 2nd, 3rd, . . .) when working with the children.*

5.4 There is a well-equipped math area with number games, countable objects, and books available daily.

7.1 All children are actively encouraged to take part in counting objects in a variety of contexts (e.g., role play, snack time, sharing LEGO).*

7.2 Adults incorporate into their planning working with children on specific number activities three or more times a week (e.g., dice games, dominoes, matching numbers to numbers or numbers to pictures). P

7.3 Activities are planned that encourage key conceptual understandings of number (e.g., one-to-one correspondence or decomposition of number, both indoors and outdoors [or outside the center]).* P

(See Notes for Clarification on next page and see page 20 for an explanation of the use of letter codes and parentheses for observations.)

Notes for Clarification

Number activities could include counting songs/rhymes; counting books; counting games; computer/interactive whiteboard programs that includes counting; use of math resources such as 5-frames, whiteboards, collections of objects, or fingers during whole group sessions. Observers should also give credit for incidental counting during play. In theory, any play activity is acceptable if adults make counting an explicit and significant part of the activity (i.e., more than a passing mention of number). Activities should be culturally and developmentally appropriate. For example, rote counting, or use of worksheets with no concrete experiences, cannot be counted as evidence of number activities. **Daily routines** are non-play-based and might include snack or lunch time, registration, putting coats on and lining up to go outside, or tidying-up time. Use of number during routine activities might include, for example, working out how many plates are needed for snack time, counting the number of children present at registration, or counting the number of steps up to the garden area when going outdoors.

1.1 Score yes if there is evidence that children have access to appropriate counting experiences in any form (i.e., during number activities or routines) less than once per week.

1.2 Score yes if there are fewer than three resources (or sets of resources) available. Resources do not need to be accessible daily to give credit. Sets must contain enough objects to be usable as part of a counting activity.

3.1 Daily math activities are not required at this level. See the definition above for examples of number activities.

5.1 Number activities must be seen during the observation to give credit for this Indicator. Give credit if at least two examples of spontaneous counting activities with groups or individual children are observed. Alternatively, give credit if there is evidence of a daily math activity that includes all children, even if you notice adults missing other incidental opportunities for math learning during the observation. The observer does not need to see examples from all categories (i.e., songs, rhymes, counting books, and games) during the observation in order to give credit. However, confirmatory evidence should be sought in the planning, records, and display to ensure that all these options are offered at some time.

5.2 At least two examples should be observed. These could take place during group time or free play. Adults must be observed encouraging the children to count.

5.3 At least one example should be observed. Look for evidence of ordinal numbers being used during everyday activities (e.g., talking about who will be first/second/third during a turn-taking game, counting through the days of the month at registration time).

7.1 To give credit at this level, staff should be looking beyond the obvious situations that lend themselves to counting and bringing number into a wide range of contexts (both formal and informal) with small groups and individuals as well as with the whole group. At least three instances should be observed in different contexts. Staff should support children's deep understanding of counting objects, supporting children to count consistently and answer the question "How many?" without error (e.g., counting different objects, touching and moving objects, starting counting in different places with one group of objects, and counting different arrangements of objects [such as arranged vertically, horizontally, in a circle, randomly]). They should concentrate on small numbers (e.g., 2–5 objects) with younger children aged 3–4 years and higher numbers (e.g., up to 10 objects) with children aged 4–5 years and possibly, if children are ready, more than 10 objects with children aged 5 years up to 6 years.

7.3 To give credit, at least three different examples of activities that explicitly encourage a key conceptual understanding (e.g., one-to-one correspondence) must be found in the sample of planning reviewed, at least one of which must relate to outdoor activities/play. You may need to ask what the children are working on. Examples of one-to-one correspondence might include giving each child a plate for snack; setting the table with a cup, plate, etc., one of each for each setting; putting one object in each section of a container (e.g., egg carton); counting individual objects into a container, ensuring each number word is associated with one object; counting and parking one trike in each parking bay. Examples of decomposition might include separating 5 objects bought in a "shop" into two bags in as many different ways as possible; singing "5 Little Ducks Went Swimming One Day" while separating out 5 toy ducks and counting how many came back, how many were still on the pond, and how many ducks there were altogether; showing 5 using fingers in as many different ways as possible; playing a game of "Make 5" with a dice with up to 5 on it or using the fingers on one hand, showing one amount and asking "How many more to make 5?"; separating 5 balls into two buckets; inviting 5 children to choose to play on the slide or on the grass and counting the combinations at each location.

Inadequate		Minimal		Good		Excellent
1	2	3	4	5	6	7

NOTE: Items 8, 9, and 10 *MUST* be assessed. After assessing these Items, you may then select *EITHER* Item 11a, Item 11b, or Item 11c. Choose the Item that is most relevant to the content of the observation or the age of the children.

Item 9: Understanding and Representing Number

See page 5 for information regarding the importance of context, talk, and concrete, pictorial, and abstract (CPA) representations.

1.1 Children do not use concrete objects when engaging in mathematical activities.* P, D, R

1.2 Children rarely talk about numbers or "How many?" in classroom discussions or during activities, play, or routines.*

1.3 Written numbers or collections of objects to count rarely appear in displays and resources.* D

3.1 Math provision includes concrete (C) objects, pictorial (P) representations (and charts where appropriate), and resources that support abstract (A) representations/numerals.* D

3.2 Children's attention is drawn to numbers and a number sequence in a variety of contexts (e.g., through games using a number track or by talking about and showing the sequence).*

3.3 Groups of objects and their equivalent numbers are shown next to each other (e.g., a number frieze showing the number 1 next to one apple, the number 2 next to two pears, etc.). D

5.1 Children are regularly encouraged to use concrete (C) objects, including fingers, to support their math understanding.* (P), (D), (R)

5.2 There are planned classroom activities that involve pictorial (P) and/or abstract (A) representations of number. Adults encourage children to recognize and draw quantities and/or numerals; they may use a variety of materials.* P, D, R

5.3 Children are encouraged to use their knowledge of number and math to extend their play and explorations—using CPA (e.g., putting the age on a birthday card, pricing items in the shop, playing number and board games, solving problems in the environment).* (P), (D), (R)

7.1 Staff support children to understand the purpose and meaning of number through talk, discussions, and meaningful contexts (e.g., using "thinking aloud strategy" about numbers, supporting children to talk about numbers individually and in groups).* (P), (D), (R)

7.2 There are planned classroom activities that incorporate representations that are concrete, pictorial, and abstract (CPA) (i.e., where children are encouraged to use concrete objects, look at and make their own drawings to represent numbers, and look at and/or write numerals).* P, D, R; N/A permitted

(See Notes for Clarification on next page and see page 20 for an explanation of the use of letter codes and parentheses for observations.)

Notes for Clarification

1.1 Score yes if there is no evidence during the observation, or in the materials, that adults draw children's attention to concrete objects while engaging in number activities. For example, they may sing number rhymes or count without using objects or show children numerals without linking them to a context (e.g., saying "There are 3" rather than "There are 3 ducks").

1.2 Score yes if numbers are not talked about during the day, such as during routines like registration, snacks/lunches, putting on two boots and two gloves to get ready to go outside, etc.

1.3 Score yes if these are not easily visible or available for the children (e.g., at eye level or large enough to see/read from a distance, in accessible baskets).

3.1 **Concrete resources** include natural resources (e.g., leaves, sticks, shells), collections of objects (e.g., buttons, beads, Unifix cubes, double-sided counters, bears, dinosaurs) to sort and count, containers for sorting and counting, including those with multiple spaces (e.g., egg cartons, chocolate trays). **Pictorial resources** include books (with pictures that could be counted and discussed); displays featuring pictures of objects that can be counted; games with cards/spinners/dice with pictures of objects of varying quantities to be matched, sorted, compared, and sequenced; and 5-frames, 10-frames, and tally charts for older children. Also included are resources to support children make their own pictorial representations of quantities of objects and numbers, such as chalk, paints, pencils, paper, and so forth. **Abstract resources** include numerals written in the environment, number shapes, and stencils; games with spinners/dice/number tracks, and so forth; drawing/writing equipment. At least five different examples of concrete resources and one of each of the pictorial and abstract resources should be accessible daily.

3.2 At least one example, including a sequence, must be observed. Adults point out/play Spot the Numbers (e.g., on clocks, dates, houses, buses, weather, weights, money, computers, TVs, roads, recipes, medicines, etc.). They draw explicit attention to a number sequence (e.g., when playing hopscotch or a board game, saying, "What number do you move to now?"; ordering a collection of numbered cards; pointing out children's positions in a line; discussing numbers in a book, on pages, on a height chart, in a recipe book; floors of a tall building; aisles in a supermarket).

5.1 Examples: Counting or finding a named number of objects; during tidy-up time matching the number and/or type of concrete objects and returning them to their original position, such as returning 5 pennies to the purse in the home corner; matching and stacking same-sized/shaped bricks together; matching the contents of the box with the picture on the front; pairing boots, gloves; putting 10 pencils in each pot, etc. When singing counting songs/rhymes and reading books, the children themselves may become the objects, or they may use their fingers or concrete objects to represent the math (e.g., when singing "One, Two, Three, Four, Five Once I Caught a Fish Alive" or "Two Fat Sausages Sizzling in a Pan" children use their fingers; when singing "Five Little Monkeys Jumping on the Bed," the children use a piece of cloth to represent the bed and 5 plastic monkeys, and the adult asks, "How many monkeys are on the bed . . . and on the floor?" at each stage in the song). Note: Rhymes may be adapted for counting up rather than down with younger children, and quantities should be suitable to the age and skills of the children (e.g., up to 3 for 3- and 4-year-olds, up to 5 for 4- and 5-year-olds, up to 10 [and possibly 20] for 5- to 6-year-olds). As children get older, the concrete representations may be less lifelike (e.g., substituting cubes for plastic monkeys). One observed example and evidence of at least two further activities each week are required.

5.2 At least one example of children being encouraged to recognize small quantities of objects (see Indicator 5.1 for quantities) and/or numerals and draw them should be observed or evident in the reviewed materials as available weekly. They may use different contexts/media (e.g., drawing in sand/corn flour/paint/paper; on computer; using number shapes and stencils; using journals [older children]). Note: Drawing/writing may be emergent and consist of small pictures, squiggles, tallies, or lines. Adults should model drawing and writing for reticent children and avoid undue pressure. Early "writing" attempts should be celebrated; adults may ask "What do you want that to mean?" while accepting all responses.

5.3 Staff enhance the environment and support children to understand that number/math is everywhere, using CPA. Examples that extend on Indicators 3.1 and 3.2: Count how many beanbags you can throw in the bucket, how many steps to the garden, how many dinosaurs fit in the castle, how many bricks needed/used; "write" a shopping list including how many of each item are needed; draw number lines on the floor for games; measure the distance a car travels down a ramp; measure the height of your tower. Set challenges to solve: How many minibeasts in the basket? How many legs do these dinosaurs have altogether? Which is the odd one out, and why? Can you sort these objects into two groups, and then, can you do it another way? Use the bricks and copy the

(continued on page 42)

pattern. Set up an obstacle course including the bridge in the photo. Vote for the book you want read. Guess how many pom-poms are in the jar. Use the cubes/draw a picture/write a number sentence telling the story of two bears who went to the woods and then along came another bear. One example must be observed and three must be available each week.

7.1 Examples of thinking aloud: Staff may count aloud snacks/paintbrushes/cards for a game, and so forth to make sure they have the right amount/enough; count the number of toys to avoid losing any; pair shoes and socks, and so forth, explaining why they are doing this and possibly inviting children to join them. They give children time to talk about numbers and support them (e.g., "I think there are 2 dogs, what do you think?" "Can you count them to make sure?") both individually and in groups. Examples of group conversations might include the number of children who like ice cream or the number who can play at the water table together, or the number who voted for one book versus the number who voted for another; or the number who made a good guess/estimation about the number of pom-poms in the jar. Staff incorporate math discussions into all aspects of the center (e.g., while reading stories, during registration and other routines, across the environment both indoors and outside). They may use numbers to count down/up to an exciting event, discuss how numerals help to organize and label resources (e.g., 2 trucks, 10 cars), on boxes, and invite children to show so many fingers as a game to play during transitions. One observed example and evidence of at least two more examples each week is required.

7.2 Activities are planned that bring together concrete, pictorial, and abstract (CPA) representations of math. Typically, first, the adult models the process and the children complete the parts that they are comfortable with (e.g., the adults/children use puppets/figures/fingers/counters, etc., to represent a story or rhyme [see also Indicator 5.1]). Second, the adult shows pictures in a book and/or draws some representations (e.g., the three little pigs) by drawing three houses/marks. Third, the adult writes the appropriate numerals and/or number sentence. After or during this time, the children are encouraged to represent the story using concrete (C) representations *and* to draw their own pictures (P) showing any changes that occurred during the story. Finally, children may write the appropriate numeral(s) or discuss what the adult has written for them (A). Please see Indicator 5.2 also. If not observed, one example of this combination of representations (CPA) should be available each week. If the children being observed are all less than 4½ years of age, N/A is permitted.

Intentionally Blank

Inadequate 1	2	Minimal 3	4	Good 5	6	Excellent 7

NOTE: Items 8, 9, and 10 *MUST* be assessed. After assessing these Items, you may then select *EITHER* Item 11a, Item 11b, or Item 11c. Choose the Item that is most relevant to the content of the observation or the age of the children.

Item 10: Math Talk and Thinking Mathematically

1.1 Children rarely take part in activities that support their mathematical language, thinking, or problem solving.* P, D, R

1.2 Staff ask children math questions that interrupt rather than extend children's learning.*

3.1 Staff talk with children using mathematically appropriate language.*

3.2 Children's mathematical interests and investigations are discussed.*

3.3 When children ask for help, staff support them in finding their own solutions.* P, D, R, Q

5.1 Staff talk about numbers as adjectives (e.g., 2 apples, 3 birds, 4 jumps, 2 claps, etc.), rather than as nouns, or use familiar contexts, stories, or rhymes to support understanding.*

5.2 Staff support children to make links to earlier experiences, especially when learning something new.* P, D, R

5.3 Staff support the beginning of problem solving and exploration by asking children what they see and what they may question or wonder.* P, D, R

5.4 Staff talk about math with the children using their interests during child-initiated activities (e.g., "Oh, you have 2 teddies having tea. This teddy also wants some tea. How many teddies do you have now?").* Q

7.1 Staff use a variety of strategies to support children to learn new mathematical vocabulary.* P, D, R, Q

7.2 Children are encouraged to articulate and/or show their mathematical thinking as staff ask questions like these: How did you do that/know? What are you planning? What is the pattern? How did you get your answer? Is there another way?* P, D, R; N/A permitted

7.3 Staff plan real-life problems in purposeful contexts for children to explore. They support understanding by providing children with concrete representations to use and support discussion and evaluation.* P, D, R; N/A permitted

7.4 Staff support parents/carers to understand the math their children are learning. P, D, R, Q

(See Notes for Clarification on next page and see page 20 for an explanation of the use of letter codes and parentheses for observations.)

Notes for Clarification

1.1 Score yes if there is no evidence during the observation, or in materials reviewed, that adults discuss children's mathematical language or thinking (see Indicator 3.1 notes and questions) or support them in problem solving (see notes on problem solving for Indicators 7.2 and 7.3).

1.2 Score yes if you see staff asking questions that require the child to shift their focus from their current interest and that obviously interrupt their thinking or appear to be above their level of comprehension. You are likely to see children move away or ignore inappropriate questions.

3.1 Score yes if you hear at least one example. Mathematically appropriate language includes characteristics of objects, such as shape; relationships between objects and sets of objects, such as "equal to" or "the same as," "more," "less," "fewer," "taller," "longer," "shorter," "smaller," "bigger," "biggest"; positional language, such as "in front of," "next to," "behind," "nearer," "under," "on top of"; classifications of sets that may be helpful later, such as "You have 2 dogs and 1 cat; you have a lot of [3] pets!" and "Oh, yes, it has 3 pointy bits or corners and 3 sides."

3.2 Evidence is not required for all children in the group, but observers should see at least one example where staff discuss children's interests in math together. Interests could focus on shape, puzzles, measurement, numbers, patterns, maps, position, and so forth.

3.3 Evidence is not required for all children in the group. To give credit, observers should find at least one example of a child asking for something (it may not be math related; e.g., "How many plates do we need? How many pennies should I have? How do I make green paint? How can I make this stick? What do I do . . . . Why is this . . . ?") and then being supported to find their own solutions. You could find the example in the materials reviewed.

5.1 Staff recognize that numbers are symbols and so are abstract, and as such do not necessarily mean anything to young children. To support their understanding, adults always pair numbers with objects and/or meaningful contexts or stories. To score yes, you would not see any adult talk about numbers without linking them to objects, contexts, or stories. You would see them talking about numbers in meaningful contexts. Examples: "How old are you? How many fingers is that? Let's count how many steps/stairs. Would you like 2 or 3 grapes? 1, 2, 3, 4, 5, once I caught a fish alive; 1, 2, buckle my shoe; 1 potato, 2 potatoes."

5.2 One example required. For example, adult reminds child of the rules of the game, especially if they have changed; adult says, "*Remember* you had two biscuits yesterday; how many have you got today? What happened yesterday? *Remember* we had the trikes, and now we have the scooters? *Remember* how we use a recipe? Do you *remember* how you solved this before?"

5.3 Staff encourage close observation by asking children "What do you see/notice?" and the formulation of questions by asking questions like "What do you wonder?" They do this informally, when a child is looking at something, or more formally by undertaking a "notice and wonder" activity. An adult provides a stimulus (e.g., showing a picture or object), and asks, "What do you notice?" and then shows interest in and accepts all answers. Later, they may encourage children to talk about the math in the stimulus. Then they ask, "What do you wonder?" and accept all answers. Younger children may need some responses and questions modeled. If not observed, at least one example should be found in the materials reviewed.

5.4 If not observed, the Indicator can be scored using a question (e.g., "How do you support children's math during child-initiated activities [free play]? Please can you give an example?")

7.1 Examples of strategies: (1) modeling its use; (2) supporting understanding using objects, visual images, and gestures; (3) showing examples of what it is and what it's not (e.g., "This is a square. This is not, because. . . ."); (4) defining the words (e.g., "taller" means bigger when we are talking about how tall something is; "equals" means the same as); (5) using synonyms (e.g., "less" means not so much or smaller) and giving simple examples (e.g., if you want less sweets, you can give some away); (6) encouraging the child to use the new word(s) in a sentence. If this is not observed on the day, at least one example must be found in the materials reviewed.

7.2 Children show their understanding and answer questions using concrete objects, drawing, and/or talk. Children are asked to reflect on their thinking and what they did. Either this should be observed or at least one example must be found in the materials reviewed. If the group of children being observed are all less than 4½ years of age, N/A is permitted.

7.3 Adults plan math problems for children (e.g., "There are three children at the sand table, but one leaves. How many are left?" or "There are two plates of biscuits, one for doll and one for teddy. Is this fair? Do they have the same?") The adult may support the children to understand the problem by slowly going through it and helping them extract information and identify the question.

(continued on page 46)

"Some children are at the sand table. How many? Then what happens?" "One child leaves." "So, what is the question?" "How many children are left at the table?" Most children think through the problem using concrete objects (e.g., a child chooses 3 cubes to represent 3 children at the table, and when one leaves the child removes 1 cube, leaving 2; sometimes called modeling) and talk. Alternative problems might include sorting objects or pictures of objects into groups, finding the odd one out, identifying or extending a pattern, or saying what is the same or different. Adults support the children in understanding the problem, modeling the problem where appropriate, and evaluating or reflecting on what they did; see Indicator 7.2. If not observed on the day, at least one example should be found in the materials reviewed. If the group of children being observed are all less than 4½ years of age, N/A is permitted.

Intentionally Blank

Inadequate 1	2	Minimal 3	4	Good 5	6	Excellent 7

NOTE: Items 8, 9, and 10 *MUST* be assessed. After assessing these Items, you may then select *EITHER* Item 11a, Item 11b, or Item 11c. Choose the Item that is most relevant to the content of the observation or the age of the children.

Item 11a: Mathematical Activities: Shape

1.1 Little evidence that children have opportunities to experience or learn about shape (e.g., shape is rarely commented on during ordinary play or daily routines; adults do not plan activities that involve shapes).* P, D, R

3.1 Some different shapes are accessible to children.* D

3.2 Shapes are named outside planned shape activities.*

3.3 Shape is an explicit part of some activities.* P, D, R

5.1 A wide variety of shapes are accessible, and adults draw children's attention to shape names (e.g., circle, square, triangle, rectangle).*

5.2 Staff draw children's attention to shape in their own work (e.g., drawings, models).*

7.1 Many activities and materials are available that encourage children to **generalize** shape across a variety of contexts (e.g., art activities, construction activities, group play arrangements, role play).* (P), (D), (R)

7.2 Activities develop and extend concepts beyond basic shapes (e.g., to include properties of 2- or 3-dimensional shapes).* P, D, R

7.3 Staff encourage children to understand the properties of different shapes (e.g., 3 sides of a triangle) and to use this understanding to solve shape puzzles and apply their knowledge to new situations.* P, D, R; N/A permitted

(See Notes for Clarification on next page and see page 20 for an explanation of the use of letter codes and parentheses for observations.)

Notes for Clarification

1.1 Score yes if no references to shape are seen during the observation and there is no evidence in planning, records, or display that shape work has been carried out in the past.

3.1 Any resources with different-shaped pieces can be counted (e.g., blocks with different-shaped pieces, shape cutters for cooking/play dough activities, shapes displayed on the wall). At least four examples should be accessible on a daily basis to give credit.

3.2 Staff members are not required to use the proper names for shapes to give credit for this Indicator; common names are acceptable (e.g., tube). Other pattern-related language is also acceptable as evidence (e.g., pointy, wavy). At least one example of staff using shape or pattern language should be observed to give credit.

3.3 Give credit if an explicit shape activity is observed. If planning, records, or display are used as evidence, at least two different examples must be found in the sample of materials reviewed.

5.1 A good selection of shape resources (five or more examples) should be accessible on a daily basis to give credit (e.g., a shape poster, a set of shape puzzles, a set of 3D shapes, a set of blocks of different shapes, a book on shapes in the book area). Others may be available but not accessible daily. A wider variety of different shapes should also be accessible than is expected in Indicator 3.1. In addition to the availability of resources, observers should hear at least two examples of adults drawing attention to shape names.

5.2 At least one example must be observed.

7.1 At least three examples must be evident on the day of the observation, although confirmatory evidence can be found in the sample of materials reviewed.

7.2 The properties of shape are important here—talk includes describing shapes, such as pointy bits, round, wavy, sides, corners, faces, etc. and/or gestures may show how sides are horizontal, vertical, perpendicular, etc. For older children, it is important to see some less typical examples of shapes (e.g., not just an equilateral triangle, but at least two other different types of triangles [scalene, isosceles, acute, right-angle, or obtuse]).

7.3 The emphasis here is on applying knowledge of shape (e.g., finding the odd one out when shown a group of triangles in different orientations and/or of different types—not just equilateral); on being able to sort shapes when shown a group of them (e.g., a square with some other rectangles and also shapes with different numbers of sides); and on building shapes/patterns using pattern blocks and/or tangrams or similar resources with support to notice patterns (e.g., two equilateral triangles put together can make a square). If the children being observed are all less than 4½ years of age, N/A is permitted.

Inadequate		Minimal		Good		Excellent
1	2	3	4	5	6	7

NOTE: Items 8, 9, and 10 *MUST* be assessed. After assessing these Items, you may then select *EITHER* Item 11a, Item 11b, or Item 11c. Choose the Item that is most relevant to the content of the observation or the age of the children.

Item 11b: Mathematical Activities: Sorting, Matching, and Comparing

1.1 Children are not encouraged to sort, match, or compare objects and materials.* P, D, R

3.1 Some items to support sorting, comparing, and/or matching are accessible.*

3.2 Children sort, compare, and/or match by at least one identifiable criterion (e.g., heavy/light or by color).* P, D, R

3.3 Staff demonstrate sorting, comparing, or matching and allow the children to participate.*

5.1 Activities occur regularly that develop and extend sorting, comparing, and matching skills (e.g., sorting by more than one criterion, sorting in different contexts, or using objects in the child's everyday environment).* (P)

5.2 Characteristics that form the basis for sorting, matching, and comparing are made explicit by the adults.*

5.3 Staff encourage children to use comparative language when sorting, matching, comparing, or measuring (e.g., big, bigger, biggest, bigger/smaller, more /less).*

7.1 Children are encouraged to identify the characteristics of sets of objects that form the basis for sorting, matching, or comparing (e.g., to explain why a set of shapes is alike by saying, "They are all circles").*

7.2 Language that explores sorting, comparing, or matching is used in a variety of contexts across a range of activities (e.g., ordering the size of the three bears; noticing who has more grapes; using words such as curlier, bigger, heavier).*

7.3 Children are encouraged to complete a sorting/matching/comparing activity and then repeat using a different criterion (including their own) as the basis for sorting/matching/comparing (e.g., arrange hats by size, then by shape).* P, D, R

(See Notes for Clarification on next page and see page 20 for an explanation of the use of letter codes and parentheses for observations.)

Notes for Clarification

1.1 Score yes if no references to sorting, matching, or comparing are seen during the observation, and there is no evidence in planning, records, or display that such work has been carried out in the past.

3.1 Examples of items that could be matched, sorted, or compared include everyday objects such as collections of natural materials (e.g., pebbles, pine cones, shells) and different-shaped or -sized resources (e.g., containers for sand/water play, blocks) as well as the more commercial counting resources such as counting bears, Unifix cubes, or sorting/matching games. At least four examples should be accessible on a daily basis to give credit.

3.2 Give credit if children are observed sorting, matching, or comparing (with or without adults) during the observation. If planning, records, or display are used as evidence, at least two different examples must be found in the sample of materials reviewed.

3.3 At least one example should be observed and must involve staff actively demonstrating or supporting sorting/matching/comparing. This might take place as part of a planned adult-led activity, or more informally with a small number of children (e.g., showing children how to sort resources when tidying up, pointing out the fact that two children have matching colored tops and encouraging them to identify others wearing the same color, encouraging a child to make a tower using only red bricks).

5.1 At least one example should be observed. Observers should also check planning for regularity ("regularly" means at least three or four times per week).

5.2 Common characteristics that form the basis of sorting, matching, and comparing include color, shape, and size. Having objects that vary by just one characteristic (e.g., color) is easier for children than having objects that vary by more than one characteristic (e.g., color and shape). Note: Size may involve individual objects but also groups of objects (e.g., 2 piles or groups of counters can be compared—"Which has more?" and "Which has less?"). They could also be matched by group size and sorted into groups of 2, 5, or 10, for example. Older children could then skip count the groups. Working with groups of objects supports children's number sense.

5.3 At least one example must be observed. The focus here is on staff encouraging *children* to use comparative language.

7.1 At least one example must be observed.

7.2 At least two different examples must be observed.

7.3 If this is not observed on the day, at least one explicit example must be seen in the sample of materials reviewed.

Inadequate		Minimal		Good		Excellent
1	2	3	4	5	6	7

NOTE: Items 8, 9, and 10 *MUST* be assessed. After assessing these Items, you may then select *EITHER* Item 11a, Item 11b, or Item 11c. Choose the Item that is most relevant to the content of the observation or the age of the children.

Item11c: Mathematical Activities: Subitizing (answering "How many?" without counting)*

See page 6 for perceptual and conceptual subitizing definitions.

1.1 Children rarely take part in activities where amounts are subitized.* P, D, R

1.2 Very few resources are available for subitizing.* P, D, R

3.1 The learning environment is organized to support subitizing groups (e.g., resources are organized in groups of 2s, 3s, 4s, 5s, and 10s; pictures of small groups of objects and charts such as 5- and 10-frames and tally charts are displayed).*

3.2 Staff point out and talk about small groups of objects in the environment, supporting subitizing rather than counting.*

5.1 Planned activities occur regularly that develop and extend subitizing, using visual, auditory, or movement skills.* (P), (D), (R)

5.2 Planned activities occur where children are encouraged to copy/draw or show subitized quantities without needing to speak.* P, D, R

5.3 Staff encourage children to play games that support subitizing (e.g., games that require dice, spinners with groups of objects on them, subitizing cards, dominoes, or games that require you to move along a number track according to the quantity of objects shown).* P, D, R

7.1 Planning shows that a variety of subitizing activities are offered (visual, auditory, and movement).* P

7.2 Subitizing activities and discussions show progression and are appropriate to the understandings of the children present.* P, D, R

(See Notes for Clarification on next page and see page 20 for an explanation of the use of letter codes and parentheses for observations.)

Notes for Clarification

Perceptual subitizing involves instantly recognizing a small collection of objects without thinking or counting.

Conceptual subitizing involves seeing patterns in different arrangements of objects and combining them. This is still fairly instantaneous as it does not involve counting (e.g., sees 5 as a collection of 2 and 3 or 4 and 1).

1.1 Score yes if there is no evidence during the observation, or in planning/records/display, that adults ask children to subitize. Typically, subitizing activities include exposing the children to a small group of objects or a picture of objects and then asking how many objects they saw (without counting).

1.2 "Very few" is 2. Subitizing resources include small groups of objects, dominoes, dice, subitizing cards (i.e., cards with small collections of objects or dots on them), etc.

3.1 To score yes, at least one example should be seen in the learning environment, for example, resources are organized in small groups, labels include groups of objects (not just numerals). Objects are organized for ease of recognition (e.g., in dice patterns or 10-frames, registration is organized using 5- or 10-frames with pictures of the children's faces or lollipop sticks, use of tally marks to show how children have voted).

3.2 To score yes, at least one example should be observed. Examples could include "Oh, look, there are 2 birds sitting on the fence." "You have 3 grapes today." "Look, 2 shoes for 2 feet." "I heard 3 bells." "You did 3 jumps." "The dice is showing 5."

5.1 At least one example of adults explicitly supporting subitizing must be observed, and then at least three other opportunities for subitizing should be found in the materials reviewed. This may take place during whole group time, during routines, or during child-initiated play. Examples could include the following: Visual—subitizing characters or other salient features in books, showing children images of groups of objects for a short time and asking "How many?", children showing how many with fingers when an adult says a number. Auditory—children listening to stones being dropped individually into a tin and then asked "How many?", children copying a very small number of drum beats on their own drums, children copying clapping patterns. Movement—copying the same number of star jumps as demonstrated by another, moving along a number track according to the number thrown with a die, sitting down when you see a particular number of objects.

5.2 Observers should look for supporting evidence in the environment, display, planning, or records that these opportunities are available (at least once every 2 weeks) so that the children show they have subitized the right amount without the need for a verbal answer (e.g., children may be asked to copy an image (such as a dice pattern) that the adult has shown using counters and a plate; or they may point to the correct answer to "How many?" when provided with a choice of visual representations). See also some examples of nonverbal responses in the notes for Indicator 5.1.

5.3 To score yes, at least one example should be observed or found in the materials reviewed. Examples could include evidence of spinners with groups of objects rather than numerals on them having been made and used; evidence of children playing games with subitizing cards (cards with groups of objects on them rather than numerals on them) where speed of recognition is important (such as Snap, War, or even Pairs); evidence of children having played games with dice or dominoes (e.g., throwing a dice and jumping that number of times or moving along a number track that amount, or looking at a domino and quickly saying how many and then filling in a 10-frame with counters for that amount—the first to fill the frame wins); or evidence of games where children subitize sounds and/or movements.

7.1 Score yes if planning demonstrates that a variety of different subitizing activities are offered, that is, one of each: visual, auditory, and movement. These can occur across the center (e.g., during adult-guided sessions, routines, child-initiated activities, and transitions). For younger children (under 4 years of age), keep the amounts small—3 or less; for up to 5-year-olds, the amounts could be up to 5; and for children who are beginning to conceptually subitize (maybe up to 6-year-olds), the amounts could be up to 10. With younger children, adults could get them to say "there are 2 birds on the bird feeder" or "there are 3 bears on the display," "2 dinosaurs they are playing with," show them 1 finger, or copy a small group of 3 or less objects with their own objects (visual); get them to copy 2 bangs on a drum, 3 claps, or tell them how many coins were dropped in a tin (auditory); or copy jumping forward twice, copy 3 steps, or tell how many jumps the adult just did (movement).

7.2 A visual subitizing progression may be as follows: With younger (aged 3 or 4 years) or less experienced children, who are still at the perceptual subitizing stage, the

(continued on page 54)

amounts should be kept small: initially 3 and under, then 4 and under. The objects, such as dots on a card, should be shown in varying orientations (initially horizontal and vertical, then diagonal and circular, and finally randomly). Adult questioning may be limited to "How many?" initially and then extended to "How did you know?" or "How did you see it?" With perceptual subitizing, adults accept children saying, "I just knew" or "I can see it." Adults support children to understand how important perceptual subitizing is by avoiding inadvertently negating the skill by asking them to check by counting (which is a different skill). **With older children (aged 4½ up to 6),** amounts can be up to 5 initially and then, when they begin to conceptually subitize, up to 10. Once children begin to conceptually subitize, the amounts of objects may be displayed in ways that support conceptual subitizing (e.g., with smaller groups of objects grouped together or with them grouped in dice patterns or in 5- or 10-frames). Children who can conceptually subitize may answer "How do you know?" or "What did you see?" questions with a discussion of the parts they could see (e.g., "I saw 5 and 2, which makes 7" or "I know there are 10 spaces on a 10-frame and there were 3 spaces without counters, so there must be 7 counters").

Intentionally Blank

Inadequate 1	2	Minimal 3	4	Good 5	6	Excellent 7

SUBSCALE 3: EMERGENT SCIENCE

NOTE: Items 12, 13, and 14 *MUST* be assessed. After assessing these Items, you may then select *EITHER* Item 15a, Item 15b, or Item 15c. Choose the Item that is most relevant to the content of the observation or the age of the children.

Item 12: Natural Materials*

Inadequate (1)	Minimal (3)	Good (5)	Excellent (7)
1.1 There is little access indoors to natural materials (fewer than three examples).	3.1 Some natural materials are accessible to the children indoors.* 3.2 Natural materials are accessible outdoors.*	5.1 Natural materials are used beyond decoration to illustrate specific concepts (e.g., planting seeds or bulbs to illustrate growth, seed dispersal).* P, D 5.2 Children are encouraged to explore the characteristics of natural materials.* 5.3 Adults show appreciation, curiosity, and/or respect for nature when with children (e.g., interest in, rather than fear or disgust for, fungi or worms).*	7.1 Children are encouraged to identify and explore a range of natural phenomena in their environment outside the center and talk about/describe them.* (P), (D) 7.2 Children are encouraged to bring natural materials into the center.* D, Q 7.3 Children are encouraged to make close observations of natural objects and/or draw them.* P, D, R

(See Notes for Clarification on next page and see page 20 for an explanation of the use of letter codes and parentheses for observations.)

Notes for Clarification

Natural materials include living things (e.g., plants, fish, hamsters, etc.), collections of natural objects (e.g., pebbles, pine cones, shells, etc.), and other natural materials such as sand and water. Materials should be in their natural state and recognizable as coming from the natural environment.

3.1 At least four different examples should be accessible daily. Others may be available but not accessible daily (e.g., those that cannot be left out for safety reasons).
3.2 At least five different examples should be accessible daily. Examples might include trees that are accessible to children, gardens/planting areas (e.g., herbs, vegetable plots), animals kept outdoors (e.g., rabbit, guinea pig).
5.1 Give credit if this is observed on the day. If evidence is taken solely from planning/display, at least two different examples should be evident in the materials reviewed. At this level, the planning should include an explicit reference to the idea/scientific concept being introduced (e.g., "observing and drawing butterflies over time to understand their life cycle" rather than "drawing butterflies").
5.2 Give credit if one or more examples are observed. This could include informal discussion (e.g., feeling the texture of a pebble found in the playground; looking at invertebrates [e.g., spiders, worms, snails] under stones), as well as planned activities (e.g., cutting up fruits to look at the seeds).
5.3 At least one example must be observed.
7.1 At least one discussion relating to natural phenomena/materials should be observed, and children should be seen to take an active role in the discussion. Planning or display evidence can be used as supporting evidence that children are encouraged to explore a range of natural phenomena (e.g., weather, mini-beasts, plants, animals, Forest School). Planning should also provide some evidence of planning for talk (e.g., key vocabulary).
7.2 Give credit if an example is observed on the day (e.g., staff set up a nature trail in the garden and encourage children to find objects for discussion at group time). Credit can also be given for recent display evidence showing children bringing natural materials into the center (e.g., a pet from home, gathering leaves in autumn). If not observed or seen in display, an open-ended question can be asked, for example: "How do you collect the natural materials for your topics and/or displays?" "Could you give me some examples of when children have brought in natural materials they were interested in?" Do not give credit unless specific examples can be provided.
7.3 Give credit if this is observed. If planning, records, or display are used, at least one example should be evident in the sample of materials reviewed (and this should be explicit enough to suggest that children have been encouraged to observe natural materials closely).

Inadequate 1	2	Minimal 3	4	Good 5	6	Excellent 7

NOTE: Items 12, 13, and 14 *MUST* be assessed. After assessing these Items, you may then select *EITHER* Item 15a, Item 15b, or Item 15c. Choose the Item that is most relevant to the content of the observation or the age of the children.

Item 13: Areas Featuring Science/Science Resources

Inadequate (1)	Minimal (3)	Good (5)	Excellent (7)
1.1 No evidence of science resources, displays, books, or activities.	3.1 Science provision includes a selection of items (e.g., magnets or magnifying glasses).*	5.1 A variety of science equipment is accessible for children to use.*	7.1 A wide range of science equipment is available.*
	3.2 Display(s) that show evidence of natural change (e.g., seasons).* D	5.2 There is evidence of collections of things with similar and/or different properties (e.g., things that roll, stretch, bounce, are made of plastic, of metal).*	7.2 A range of reference materials is available, including books, pictures, reference charts, and photographs.* D
	3.3 Display(s) that could be used to generate discussion about science in the world around us are visible to the children (e.g., posters of the body, life cycle of a butterfly).* D	5.3 Print resources go beyond story books to some reference books or material on science topics.*	7.3 A large and stimulating science area is set up for the children to use daily.
			7.4 Science materials feature in other areas of the center as well as the one set aside for science.*

(See Notes for Clarification on next page and see page 20 for an explanation of the use of letter codes and parentheses for observations.)

Notes for Clarification

3.1 At least two examples should be accessible on a daily basis.

3.2 The intention of this Indicator is that adults have made an effort to "bring the outdoors in" and/or provide an opportunity for children to consider changes in the natural world.

3.3 The display must have a science purpose (e.g., posters showing pets or a generic woodland scene would not be adequate).

5.1 Variety means more of each type of item (so that several children can use the materials at once), but also a greater variety of items than is required for Indicator 3.1. At least five different examples should be accessible daily to give credit. Only give credit for general sand and water materials (e.g., funnels/containers/plastic tubes) if there is evidence that these are used for the learning of science, for example, exploring sinking and floating.

5.2 There must be evidence that collections have been put together on the basis of their scientific properties and not, for example, because they are all the same color. Collections do not need to be accessible daily.

5.3 At least four examples (e.g., four science books) should be accessible daily to give credit.

7.1 As required for Indicator 5.1, plus examples of more specialized science materials that relate to specific topics (e.g., color [colored lenses, color paddles], light [prisms, light boxes], electricity [batteries, wires]). These more specialized items do not need to be accessible to the children on a daily basis.

7.2 Examples of all four categories should be available within the center and easily accessible to adults so that they can refer to them when needed. A smaller range (representing several of the categories) should be accessible to the children daily. Pictures might include posters or other displays.

7.4 For example, a seaside role play area supplemented with reference books on seaside creatures, a crab claw, and a magnifying glass so that the children can make close observations.

Inadequate		Minimal		Good		Excellent
1	2	3	4	5	6	7

NOTE: Items 12, 13, and 14 *MUST* be assessed. After assessing these Items, you may then select *EITHER* Item 15a, Item 15b, or Item 15c. Choose the Item that is most relevant to the content of the observation or the age of the children.

For this Item, look for evidence of engaging children in scientific processes (i.e., close observation, raising questions/making guesses [hypothesizing], experimenting [seeing what happens], and communicating and interpreting results [why has this happened?]). NOTE: Indicators 7.4 and 7.5 may not be applicable (N/A) unless there are older children in the group.

Item 14: Developing Scientific Thinking and the Scientific Process*

1.1 Questions raised by children are often ignored, especially if unrelated to the current activity.

1.2 Staff do not get involved in child-initiated activities/discussions.

1.3 During routine activities (e.g., story time/tray play/toy play/continuous play), there is no discussion about the materials used in the activity.*

1.4 Materials used in tray/toy play appear randomly chosen.*

3.1 Staff respond to questions in a respectful way even when they are unrelated to the immediate activity (e.g., they do not dismiss questions out of hand).

3.2 Staff involve themselves in child-initiated activities, but questions are mostly superficial or instructional.*

3.3 Routine activities are used to draw children's attention to the basic properties of materials used.*

3.4 Materials used in tray/toy/continuous/routine play appear to have been chosen to pique children's interests.*

5.1 Staff recognize the social dimension of inquiry and open questions from one child to their play partner(s) or the wider group.*

5.2 Staff immerse themselves in a child-initiated activity and use this to pose questions that lead children to consider their surroundings and formulate a hypothesis.* P, D, R, Q

5.3 Adults use routine activities to pose questions that lead children to consider their surroundings and formulate a hypothesis.* P, D, R, Q

7.1 Staff stand back from giving immediate answers to questions, but allow children to elaborate on their thinking and engage other children in their thoughts and prediction processes.*

7.2 Adults help children act on a hypothesis and conduct an investigation.* P, D, R, Q

7.3 Adults discuss the results of the investigation with children and relate the findings back to the hypothesis. P, D, R, Q

For older children (4½ to 6)*

7.4 Adults work with children to record their (1) hypothesis, (2) test, and (3) results of their investigation.* P, D, R, Q; N/A permitted

7.5 Adults work with children to report back on and evaluate their results (which may lead to further questions and investigations).* P, D, R, Q; N/A permitted

(See Notes for Clarification on next page and see page 20 for an explanation of the use of letter codes and parentheses for observations.)

Notes for Clarification

The purpose of this item is to demonstrate that adults engage children (age appropriately) with the scientific process: observing, questioning, hypothesizing, investigating (testing), recording, and discussing results. It also relates to the adult's intentional pedagogy in using child-initiated or routine activities to guide children through the scientific process, with credit given incrementally to reflect the whole process. The lowest score is given if staff do not encourage questioning and curiosity. A minimal score suggests adults acknowledge children's questions and use routine activities to pique children's interest. For good practice, staff must intentionally use child-initiated or routine activities to help children develop meaningful questions leading to a hypothesis that could reasonably be answered/investigated. Highest scores are awarded if staff help children to investigate (test) their hypothesis. With older children, the observer should look for evidence that the results of an investigation have been recorded and discussed, as this can provide opportunities for further questioning/investigations. At the higher end of the scale, the observer may not see the whole range on the day, so it is important that there is sufficient time to look for evidence either in displays, questioning the adult, or looking through activity/session/lesson plans.

1.3, 1.4 See **Examples of Everyday Routines** in the next column.

3.2 If a child is playing with toy cars, the adult may ask, "Which car do you like the best?" without asking for an explanation from the child as to what it is about this car that makes it a favorite, or "Can you put the cars in a line?" This kind of questioning would gain credit at this level.

3.3, 3.4 Example of drawing attention to basic properties: "Which cars are made of plastic? Which cars are made of metal?" See **Examples of Everyday Routines** in the next column. One observed example per indicator is sufficient here.

5.1 Note: One observed example is required for Indicator 5.1 and for Indicators 5.2 and 5.3; if not observed on the day, then at least one example must be found in the materials reviewed.

5.2 A child has sneakers that light up when they walk. The adult says, "Wow, your shoes light up, but mine don't. Why do you think that happens? How could we find out what makes some shoes light up and not others?" One observed example is needed.

5.3 See **Examples of Everyday Routines** in the next column.

7.1 Must be observed. For other Indicators at Level 7, if not observed on the day, then at least one example must be found in the materials reviewed.

7.2 Some examples to illustrate credit: "So you think the car will go faster on the wooden floor than on the carpet? How should we do this? What do we need to do to find out if this is true?"

7.4, 7.5 If the group of children observed are less than 4½ years of age, N/A is permitted.

Examples of Everyday Routines Being Used to Engage Children in the Science Process

Story Time: Adult uses story books to introduce scientific concepts such as the strength of materials (*3 Little Pigs*, *Room on the Broom*), or a book may have been chosen to deliberately introduce a scientific concept (e.g., ice cream melting, effects of the weather, light and dark). At the end of the story, the adult poses open questions about the story (e.g., Why was the stick house stronger than the straw house?) and allows discussion. The adult may have props relevant to the story (straw, stick, bricks) to promote interest and stimulate questions about how children could test their ideas about the science in the story.

Tray Play: Give low scores if at the water/sand/messy tray children experience only a selection of random materials chosen without any apparent learning intention evident or adult support for learning. Note: Messy trays can contain rice, cereal, corn flour, foam, etc. Score minimal if the objects in the tray have been chosen to allow an exploration of the tray's base material (e.g., floaters and sinkers, waterwheels, holed containers that allow substances to flow through at different speeds, different-sized/shaped/colored containers, etc.). Score good if staff draw attention to how the objects act/interact and ask children to predict/record what might occur (e.g., What sinks quickest? How can the waterwheel be made to move quicker/slower? What happens if we add water to the sand/seeds/corn flour, etc.? How does it feel before/after we add the water? Do you think it would be the same if we used hotter water, wet/dry sand, colored water, etc.?).

Toy/Continuous Play: Give low scores if children are not afforded opportunities to investigate the properties of their toys or materials used in continuous provision (e.g., paints, glue, etc.). Score minimal if the adult encourages children to explore their toys/continuous provision materials (e.g., looking at similarities, differences, and changes). What is this made of? What else is made of this material? What does it feel like? What does it smell like? Is it light or heavy? How fast does it move? Score good if adults pose questions that encourage children to question and make predictions. The highest scores are given when an investigation has been conducted and, with older children, when there is evidence of recording and the evaluation of results: So what did we find out? Were we right in what we guessed would happen? What would happen if we tried this again but with . . . (change a variable)?

Inadequate		Minimal		Good		Excellent
1	2	3	4	5	6	7

NOTE: Items 12, 13, and 14 *MUST* be assessed. After assessing these Items, you may then select *EITHER* Item 15a, Item 15b, or Item 15c. Choose the Item that is most relevant to the content of the observation or the age of the children.

Item 15a: Science Activities: Nonliving

Inadequate

1.1 Children are not encouraged to explore aspects of their physical environment, and scientific words and concepts do not feature in discussions.* P, D, R

Minimal

3.1 A few science explorations or experiments are carried out by adults or children (e.g., ice cubes put out in the sun).* P, D, R

3.2 Scientific words and/or concepts are mentioned (e.g., discussing the weather; using the words "floating" and "sinking" at the water tray; talking about melting, pressure, why/how things move).* D

Good

5.1 Staff often plan and introduce appropriate scientific concepts (e.g., how materials change, magnetism, sinkers and floaters) and children handle materials.* P, D, R

5.2 Adults draw attention to characteristics or changes in materials (e.g., birthday candles melting).*

5.3 Children are encouraged to use more than one sense to explore nonliving phenomena and talk about their experience (e.g., touch/smell as well as sight).*

Excellent

7.1 Children have hands-on experience in varied science activities exploring nonliving materials.* (P), (D), (R)

7.2 Children are encouraged to experience a range of scientific concepts/ideas.* P, D, R

7.3 Adults engage children in discussion about materials and their characteristics.*

7.4 Adults encourage children to ask questions.*

7.5 Adults support children in systematically seeking answers to questions.*

7.6 Children are encouraged to record results of scientific inquiry.* P, D, R; N/A permitted

(See Notes for Clarification on next page and see page 20 for an explanation of the use of letter codes and parentheses for observations.)

Notes for Clarification

1.1 Score yes if no examples are observed and no evidence is found in the planning/records/display reviewed.

3.1 Give credit if this is observed. If planning, records, or display are used as evidence, at least two different examples must be found in the sample of materials reviewed. Examples might include investigating the friction of different surfaces for toy cars, or the insulation/absorbency properties of different materials (e.g., "Which material will keep our doll the warmest/driest?").

3.2 At least one example must be observed and must relate to nonliving processes. This could take place during a planned science activity, or during everyday/informal activities or play.

5.1 This Indicator requires that staff plan for science learning. At least four different examples relating to nonliving processes must be found in the sample of materials (planning, records, and display) reviewed. At this level, the planning should include an explicit reference to the idea/scientific concept being introduced (e.g., "investigating which materials are magnetic and nonmagnetic" rather than "magnet play"). The second part of the Indicator requires that children have the opportunity to handle materials (i.e., that staff do not simply demonstrate experiments for children to watch).

5.2 Adults must be observed drawing attention either to characteristics or to change at least once to give credit (e.g., drawing attention to water evaporating from the ground on a hot day). At this level, the talk should be more scientific than is required for Indicator 3.2.

5.3 At least one example must be observed to give credit. As well as being encouraged to use more than one sense, children should also be encouraged to talk about their experience using descriptive language (e.g., "What does it smell like?").

7.1 In order to assess whether activities are introduced in a hands-on way, at least one science activity must have been observed (e.g., exploring magnets and magnetic objects)—although not all children need to have taken part on that day. Evidence from planning, records, and display should also be reviewed to assess the variety in "nonliving" activities provided (and this evidence should also point to a hands-on approach for all children).

7.2 In order to give credit, a broader range of concepts and ideas should be evident in the materials reviewed than is required for Indicator 5.1. Possible science nonliving topics to discuss and explore:

(1) sorting and classifying materials by various properties, such as type: including metal, plastic, wood, paper, glass, rock, water, air; or by senses: including hard, soft, rough, smooth, heavy, light, springy, firm, shiny, or dull; or by state and changes within those: solid, liquid, gas

(2) looking at and discussing forces, such as staying still or starting to move, speeding up or slowing down, changing direction, changing shape, gravity

(3) deliberate explorations of air and water, such as wind, pneumatic toys, balloons, bubbles, bicycle pumps, air in water and the water cycle, surface tension, absorbent materials, floating, and sinking

(4) considering magnets and magnetism, such as looking at their use, working out what is magnetic in the environment, how strong a set of magnets are, and making magnets

(5) exploring electricity, such as looking at its uses, then experimenting with battery-operated toys and flashlights, simple circuits, and motors

(6) experimenting with sound, investigating how we hear, what echoes are, exploring musical instruments, volume and pitch

(7) playing with light and shadow and colors, such as how we see, transparent, translucent and opaque, rainbows, light and dark, mixing different-colored lights and paints, mirrors and reflective surfaces, shadows inside and out

(8) astronomy and the earth, including looking at the earth, moon, solar system, tides, night and day, seasons, weather, rocks, sand, and clay

7.3, 7.4, 7.5 At least one example must be observed, but one or more high-quality interactions may provide examples of Indicators 7.3, 7.4, and/or 7.5.

7.6 N/A permitted when all children in the group are younger than 4½ years of age.

Inadequate 1	2	Minimal 3	4	Good 5	6	Excellent 7

NOTE: Items 12, 13, and 14 *MUST* be assessed. After assessing these Items, you may then select *EITHER* Item 15a, Item 15b, or Item 15c. Choose the Item that is most relevant to the content of the observation or the age of the children.

Item 15b: Science Activities: Living Processes

NOTE: All safety precautions and respect must be undertaken when handling anything living.

1.1 Children are not encouraged to explore aspects of their natural environment, and scientific words and concepts do not feature in discussions.* P, D, R

1.2 Adults demonstrate unsafe hygiene practices with living creatures (e.g., not washing their hands, not getting children to wash their hands after handling animals/pets, not wiping tables after animals have been on them, allowing animals near children's food, etc.).

3.1 A few science explorations or experiments are carried out by adults or children (e.g., growing seedlings, keeping tadpoles).* P, D, R

3.2 Scientific words and concepts are mentioned (e.g., plant growth, insect habitats, the cycle of life, caring for living things).*

3.3 There are living things present, either indoors or outdoors (e.g., plants, fish, snails).

3.4 Staff demonstrate some knowledge of hygiene practices, but these are applied inconsistently (e.g., they may get children to wash their hands, but don't check them; they may wash their own, but not wipe down tables).

5.1 Staff often plan and introduce appropriate scientific concepts and children handle materials.* P, D, R

5.2 Adults draw attention to characteristics or changes in the natural world (e.g., the life cycle of a butterfly, the aging process, the different parts of a flower).*

5.3 Children are encouraged to use more than one sense to explore living phenomena and talk about their experience (e.g., touch, smell, as well as sight).*

5.4 Staff demonstrate good knowledge of hygiene and apply this consistently.

7.1 All children have hands-on experience with living things where appropriate.* (P), (D), (R)

7.2 Children are encouraged to experience a range of scientific concepts/ideas.* P, D, R

7.3 Adults engage the children in discussion about both plant and animal worlds and their characteristics.*

7.4 Adults encourage children to ask questions.*

7.5 Adults support children in systematically seeking answers to questions.*

7.6 Children without prompts wash their hands after handling living creatures, or when the educator says, "What do we do after handling creatures?" they say "Wash our hands."

7.7 Children are encouraged to record results of scientific inquiry.* P, D, R; N/A permitted

(See Notes for Clarification on next page and see page 20 for an explanation of the use of letter codes and parentheses for observations.)

Notes for Clarification

1.1 Score yes if no examples are observed and no evidence is found in the planning, records, and display reviewed.

3.1 Give credit if this is observed. If planning, records, or display are used as evidence, at least two different examples relating to living processes must be found in the sample of materials reviewed.

3.2 At least one example must be observed and must relate to living processes. This could take place during a planned science activity or during everyday/informal activities or play. Examples might include discussing pets owned by the children or looking at a spider found in the playground.

5.1 This Indicator requires that staff plan for science learning. At least four different examples relating to living processes must be found in the sample of materials (planning, records, and display) reviewed. At this level, the planning should include an explicit reference to the idea/scientific concept being introduced (e.g., "observing and drawing butterflies over time to understand their life cycle" rather than "drawing butterflies"). The second part of the Indicator requires that children have the opportunity to handle materials (i.e., that staff do not simply demonstrate experiments for children to watch).

5.2 Adults must be observed drawing attention either to characteristics or to change at least once to give credit. At this level, the talk should be more scientific than is required for Indicator 3.2.

5.3 At least one example must be observed to give credit. As well as being encouraged to use more than one sense, children should also be encouraged to talk about their experience using descriptive language (e.g., What does it feel like?).

7.1 In order to assess whether activities are introduced in a hands-on way, at least one science activity must have been observed (e.g., planting seeds, hunting for and collecting invertebrates [e.g., spiders, worms, snails]), although not all children need to be observed taking part. Evidence from planning, records, and display should also be reviewed to assess the variety in "living processes" activities provided (and this evidence should also point to a hands-on approach for all children).

7.2 In order to give credit, a broader range of concepts and ideas should be evident in the materials reviewed than is required for Indicator 5.1. Possible science living topics to discuss and explore: (1) Plants/trees (flora): Sorting and classifying leaves/flowers by properties such as shape, color, or texture; hard, soft, rough, smooth, shiny, dull; or by senses, including heavy, light, springy, firm, and fragrant. Conditions for growth. What happens if they are put in the dark/the fridge or not watered? Keeping growth charts. What happens when plants decay? Which plants can be eaten and which cannot? Why we can't eat some plants and what might happen if we do eat some (poisonous) plants? (2) Animals (fauna): Exploration and discussions can include both center pets (guinea pig, fish, etc.) and outdoor invertebrates (e.g., spiders, worms, snails). Basic classification: Insects, mammals, etc. and their properties. What do they all have in common? What are their differences? What do different animals like to eat? How do they eat/excrete? What do these different animals need to stay healthy? Keeping growth charts. Looking closely at change (e.g., tadpoles into frogs, etc.).

7.3 To give credit, at least one example of discussion relating to the plant world, and one to the animal world, must be observed.

7.3, 7.4, 7.5 At least one example must be observed, but one or more high-quality interactions may provide examples of Indicators 7.3, 7.4, and 7.5.

7.7 N/A permitted when all children in the group are younger than 4½ years of age.

Inadequate		Minimal		Good		Excellent
1	2	3	4	5	6	7

NOTE: Items 12, 13, and 14 *MUST* be assessed. After assessing these Items, you may then select *EITHER* Item 15a, Item 15b, or Item 15c. Choose the Item that is most relevant to the content of the observation or the age of the children.

Item 15c: Science Activities: Food Preparation*

1.1 No preparation of food or drink is undertaken with the children.* P, D, R, Q

1.2 Adults demonstrate unsafe hygiene practices before handling food (e.g., not washing their hands, not getting children to wash their hands before cooking, not wiping tables before handling food).

3.1 Food preparation is sometimes undertaken with the children.* P, D, R, Q

3.2 Some children have the opportunity to participate in food preparation.* P, D, Q

3.3 Some food-related discussion takes place where appropriate (e.g., staff and children talk about food at snack time or during a cooking activity).*

3.4 Staff demonstrate some knowledge of hygiene practices, but these are applied inconsistently (e.g., they may get children to wash their hands, but not check them; they may wash their own hands, but not wipe down tables).

5.1 Food preparation/cooking activities are often provided.* P, D, R, Q

5.2 Most of the children have the opportunity to participate in food preparation.* P, D, R, Q

5.3 The staff lead discussion about the food involved and use appropriate language (e.g., melt, dissolve).*

5.4 Children are encouraged to use more than one sense (e.g., feel, smell, taste) to explore individual ingredients and talk about their experiences.*

5.5 Staff demonstrate good knowledge of hygiene and apply this consistently.

7.1 A variety of cooking activities (in which all children have the opportunity to take part) is often provided. P

7.2 The end result is admired, edible, and valued (e.g., eaten by children, taken home).

7.3 The staff lead and encourage discussion on the process of food preparation and/or question children about it (e.g., "What did it look like before? What does it look like now? What has happened to it?").*

7.4 Children without prompts wash their hands before handling food or when the educator asks "What do we do before we cook?" they say, "Wash our hands."

(See Notes for Clarification on next page and see page 20 for an explanation of the use of letter codes and parentheses for observations.)

Notes for Clarification

Food preparation includes cooking activities and also the preparation of food for snack or meal time (which children may observe or participate in).

1.1 Score yes if children do not have the opportunity to observe (or participate) in food preparation/cooking during the observation, or if there is no evidence in the planning, records, and display reviewed that children are ever offered this experience, and (when asked) staff are not able to provide examples of such activities taking place.

3.1 This might include children observing a member of staff preparing food. If planning, records, or display are used as evidence, at least two examples must be found in the sample of materials reviewed.

3.2 This may be spontaneous (e.g., some children helping to prepare food for snack or lunch time) or planned in advance (e.g., planned cooking activities). If planning, records, or display are used as evidence, at least two examples must be found in the sample of materials reviewed.

3.3 At least one example must be observed. Examples at snack or meal time might include a discussion about burned toast, new cookies, or food brought in by the children.

5.1, 5.2 "Often" here means once every 2 weeks (or more frequently). Credit can be given at Indicator 5.1 if food preparation activities are offered once every 2 weeks (even if not all children have a chance to participate this frequently). To give credit at Indicator 5.2, most children (over 50%) should have an opportunity to take part in food preparation at least once every 2 weeks.

5.3 This must be observed at least once. At this level, the talk should be more scientific than is required for Indicator 3.3 (e.g., "Why did the toast get burned?").

5.4 At least one example must be observed. As well as being encouraged to use more than one sense, children should also be encouraged to talk about their experience using descriptive language (e.g., "What does it smell like?").

7.3 This must be observed at least once. Children must be actively involved in the discussion, and staff should be observed supporting and scaffolding the children's scientific language and learning.

Inadequate		Minimal		Good		Excellent
1	2	3	4	5	6	7

SUBSCALE 4: SUPPORTING DIVERSITY AND INCLUSION

Item 16: Planning for and Supporting Individual Learning Needs (Ask to see the planning and the records kept on individual children.)

1.1 Activities and resources are not matched to different ages, developmental stages, or interests.* P, Q

1.2 Planning for a diverse range of children's needs is not written down.* P

1.3 Written planning takes no account of specific individuals or groups. P

1.4 No records kept, or if records are kept, they describe activities rather than the child's response or success in that activity (e.g., ticked developmental checklists or samples of children's work with note on age/date). R

3.1 Some additional provision is made in terms of developmental stage, or for individuals or groups with specific needs such as learning support or English language support.* P, Q

3.2 Some of the written planning shows differentiation for particular individuals or groups.* P

3.3 Written records indicate some awareness of how individuals have coped with activities, or of the appropriateness of activities (e.g., needs bilingual support, able to count to 2).* R

3.4 Staff show some awareness of the need to support and recognize children's differences, praising children of all abilities publicly.*

3.5 Books, pictures, Small World figures, dolls, and/or displays show positive images of disabled people and people with additional learning needs. D

5.1 The range of activities provided draws on children's interests and caters for all developmental stages and backgrounds, enabling all children in the group to participate in a satisfying and cognitively demanding way.* P, Q

5.2 Day-to-day plans are drawn up with the specific aim of developing activities that will satisfy the interests and needs of each child, either individually or as groups.* P

5.3 Children are observed frequently, and individual records are kept on their progress in different aspects of their development.* R

5.4 Staff consistently draw children's attention to similarities and differences in a positive way.* (D)

5.5 Staff intervene appropriately when a child or an adult in the center shows prejudice.* Q

7.1 The organization of social interaction enables children of all developmental stages/backgrounds to participate at an appropriate level in both individual/common tasks (e.g., pairing children of different ages and abilities for certain tasks).* Q

7.2 Planning identifies the role of the adult when working with individuals/pairs/groups of children. It also shows a range of capability levels at which a task or activity may be experienced.* P

7.3 Observations and records of progress are used to inform planning.* P, R, Q

7.4 Staff specifically plan activities that draw the attention of the whole group to similarities, differences, and capabilities in a positive way (e.g., showing disabled children in a positive light; pointing out that *all* our bodies have skin, blood, hair, etc.; or celebrating bilingualism).* P, D, R

7.5 Staff are confident in discussing and challenging the stereotypical behaviors and assumptions of children.* Q

(See Notes for Clarification on next page and see page 20 for an explanation of the use of letter codes and parentheses for observations.)

Notes for Clarification

Activities and Planning

1.1, 3.1, 5.1, 1.2, 3.2, 5.2 There should be evidence that differentiated activities and/or resources are offered to children with particular needs (e.g., English Language Learners [ELL]) and according to age and developmental stage.

1.1, 3.1, 5.1 These Indicators relate to the provision/adaptation of activities and resources offered to children (whether these are planned or informal) and the extent to which these cater for differing needs.

1.2, 3.2, 5.2 These Indicators specifically assess the extent to which differentiation is *planned for*.

5.1, 5.2 The range of activities should provide for all children (e.g., children of different ages/stages, children with English as an additional language, Indigenous children, children with Special Educational Needs or Disabilities (SEND), and children with additional learning needs, and/or disabled children).

7.1 It may be necessary to ask about this as it will not always be apparent why children have been encouraged to work together on a task. For example: "Why have you encouraged those children to work together?" or "Do you ever encourage particular children to work together? Why? Can you give some examples?"

7.2 Adult guidance should be more detailed than simply listing which adult works with which activity/group. Both elements of the Indicator (i.e., the adult guidance and the range of capability levels) must be met in order to give credit.

Observations and Record Keeping

3.3 Credit can be given for records/observations that show fairly minimal awareness of how individuals have coped with activities (or of the appropriateness of activities).

5.3 For credit, children should be observed weekly (or almost weekly) in some form. This may take the form of Post-it notes recording specific incidents or achievements rather than formal observations. Records of progress do not need to be updated weekly.

7.3 It may be necessary to ask a question to establish whether this happens (for example, ask staff to provide or show specific examples of observations being used to inform planning).

Recognizing and Supporting Differences and Similarities

3.4 Give credit if it is clearly part of usual practice to praise all children in the group regularly.

5.4 This relates to discussing differences and similarities in a positive way. To give credit, the discussion must be more specific than is required for Indicator 3.4 (e.g., drawing specific attention to a new skill a child has mastered, a sensitive discussion with the group at lunch time about why particular children don't eat meat, explaining in an appropriate way why a disabled child sits on a special chair or why a child with autism might exhibit certain behaviors). At least one example must be observed, and supporting evidence may also be found in display (e.g., children's work displayed with specific comments about their achievements).

5.5 This relates to prejudice against children with additional learning needs and/or disabled children (e.g., talking about children's abilities [and the abilities of others] in front of children, expressing pity, being overprotective, or seeing difference as problematic and defining the child). It may be necessary to ask a question (e.g., "What would you do if one of the children or adults showed prejudice against a disabled child or a child with additional learning needs?"). Give credit for this Indicator if the answer indicates a sensitive approach: The person should not be blamed, but told that their words and/or behavior are inappropriate/inaccurate. The adult should then provide a correct explanation and suggest a more appropriate response.

7.4 This goes beyond the children in the group to consider the celebration of difference and similarities more generally. Observers should check planning for evidence that discussions of difference, similarity, and capability are specifically planned for (e.g., discussing blindness and deafness as part of a topic on senses). Evidence may also be found in display or in children's records. To give credit, at least one example of explicit planning for discussions of similarities and difference should be found in the materials reviewed.

7.5 If not observed, you can score using a question (e.g., "What would you do if a child with additional learning needs was consistently cast as the 'baby' during role play or not allowed to join play, e.g., told not to paint because they could not see well?"). Alternatively, the observer might ask for examples of occasions when children have said something "disablist" or excluded children with additional learning needs and how this was dealt with. Unless a very specific answer is given to any question asked, this Indicator should be scored based on what is observed.

Inadequate 1	2	Minimal 3	4	Good 5	6	Excellent 7

Item 17: Gender Equality and Awareness

Inadequate (1)

1.1 Where books, pictures, Small World figures, dolls, and/or displays portray gender, few of them challenge gender stereotypes.* D

1.2 The staff ignore or encourage stereotyped gender behaviors (e.g., only girls are praised for looking pretty or boys for being strong).*

Minimal (3)

3.1 Some books, pictures, Small World figures, dolls, and/or displays that challenge gender stereotypes are accessible to the children (e.g., father looking after baby, female soldier, photos of both boys and girls playing with the large blocks).* D

3.2 Children's activities and behavior sometimes cross gender stereotypes (e.g., boys cooking or caring for dolls in the home corner, girls playing outside on large mobile toys).

3.3 Some materials show examples of different types of families (e.g., single parent, blended, extended, or same-sex).

Good (5)

5.1 Many books, pictures, Small World figures, dolls, and/or displays show males and females in non-stereotypical roles (e.g., male childcare worker, woman changing a tire).* D

5.2 Participation in activities that cross gender boundaries is common practice and/or adults explicitly encourage this where necessary (e.g., all children are expected—but not forced—to join in construction and dance).* (Q)

5.3 Dressing-up clothes encourage nonstereotyped cross-gender roles (e.g., unisex nurse or police outfits; nongendered clothing such as overalls).* (P), (Q)

Excellent (7)

7.1 The children's attention is specifically drawn to books, pictures, Small World figures, dolls, and/or displays that show males and females in nonstereotypical roles, and/or specific activities are developed to help the children discuss gender.* P, Q

7.2 Staff are confident in discussing and challenging the stereotypical behaviors and assumptions of children.* Q

7.3 Male educators are employed to work with children, and/or males are sometimes invited to work in the center with the children.* Q

(See Notes for Clarification on next page and see page 20 for an explanation of the use of letter codes and parentheses for observations.)

Notes for Clarification

1.1 Only score yes if there is very little (or no) evidence of resources that counter stereotypes (e.g., less than 1 in 10 [10%] of resources that portray gender). Credit can be given for resources of one type if these are plentiful enough (e.g., many books but no pictures, Small World figures, dolls, or displays).

1.2 Only score yes if several examples (or one very explicit example) of stereotyping or of staff ignoring stereotypical behavior/comments are seen during the observation.

3.1 Overall, 10% (or more) of the resources that portray gender should be non-stereotypical to give credit. Examples from two of the five categories should be evident and accessible to children on a daily basis.

5.1 Overall, 20% (or more) of the accessible resources that portray gender should be nonstereotypical to give credit. Examples from three of the five categories should be evident and accessible on a daily basis (although many examples in every category are not required).

5.2 Observers should look for evidence that all children access activities and areas that might be associated with one gender (e.g., woodworking bench, playing with dolls in the home corner, active gross motor play). If this is seen to be common practice, credit can be given. If, however, one gender appears to dominate a particular activity to the exclusion of others and staff do not act to address this (e.g., by encouraging boys to join play in the home corner), then score down. It may be necessary to ask a question to discover any particular strategies employed (e.g., if certain times are set aside for girls to play on very active gross motor equipment). However, unless a very specific answer is given to any question asked, this Indicator should be scored based on observed behavior of children and staff.

5.3 If appropriate dressing-up resources are seen to be available but are stored so that they are not accessible to children daily, the observer should check planning or ask a question to discover how often they are made accessible. Give credit if dressing-up clothes that encourage nongendered roles are accessible to children twice a week or more.

7.1 Give credit if one or more examples are observed. Observable examples might include staff reading and discussing stories like *The Paperbag Princess* or *Mrs. Plug the Plumber*, which challenge traditional role models. If nonstereotypical books and resources are present but adults are not observed using them, ask a non-leading question such as "Did you choose these resources for a particular reason?" or "Could you give me an example of how you use these books/resources?" Credit can also be given if explicit evidence is found in the planning of activities to help children discuss gender (at least one example in the sample of planning reviewed).

7.2 If this is not observed, the Indicator may be scored using a question (e.g., "What would you do if a child suggested girls were not allowed to play with the tools because "Fixing things is a man's job?" or if a group of children were excluding a child because they did not conform to their view of how boys/girls should be [e.g., they dressed differently]?"). Alternatively, the observer might ask for examples of occasions when children have said something "sexist" and how this was dealt with. Unless a very specific answer is given to any question asked, this Indicator should be scored based on what is observed.

7.3 If male educators are not employed to work with the children, credit can be given if men are invited into the center to take part in activities with the children at least three times per year.

Inadequate 1	2	Minimal 3	4	Good 5	6	Excellent 7

Item 18: Race Equality and Awareness

Inadequate (1)

1.1 Books, pictures, Small World figures, dolls, and displays show little evidence of ethnic diversity in our society or the wider world.* D

1.2 Negative, stereotyped, or offensive images are on view to the children (e.g., a golliwog, Red Indians). D

1.3 In countries with Indigenous populations, there is no representation visible in the resources (e.g., no books or toys, or only negative representation).* N/A permitted

Minimal (3)

3.1 The children sometimes play with toys, resources, or materials from cultures other than the ethnic majority.* P, D, R

3.2 Books, pictures, Small World figures, dolls, and/or displays show people from a variety of Indigenous and/or ethnic groups.* D

Good (5)

5.1 Children play with toys, resources, or materials drawn from a range of cultures (e.g., range of appropriate and nonstereotypical dressing-up clothes, cooking and eating utensils used in dramatic play, musical instruments).* (P)

5.2 Some books, pictures, Small World figures, dolls, and/or displays show people from Indigenous and/or ethnic groups in nonstereotypical roles (e.g., as scientists, doctors, engineers, office workers in suits).* D

5.3 Some images or activities show children that they have much in common with people from other cultural groups (e.g., images that stress physical similarities or similarities in rituals and day-to-day activities).* P, D

5.4 Staff intervene appropriately when a child or an adult in the center shows prejudice.*

Excellent (7)

7.1 Staff develop activities with the express purpose of promoting cultural understanding (e.g., attention is drawn to similarities and differences in things and people, different cultures are routinely brought into topic work, visitors and performers reflect a range of cultures).* P, D, R, Q

7.2 Specific activities are developed to promote understanding of difference (e.g., paints are mixed to match skin tones to visibly show subtlety in differences).* P, D, R, Q

7.3 Minority ethnic/Indigenous educators are employed in the center, and/or Black and minority ethnic/Indigenous people are sometimes invited into the center to work with the children. Q

(See Notes for Clarification on next page and see page 20 for an explanation of the use of letter codes and parentheses for observations.)

Notes for Clarification

1.1, 3.1, 5.1 Resources should be clearly visible and in areas frequently used by the children.
1.3 Not applicable in countries with non-Indigenous peoples.
3.1 At this level the resources may not be out every day, but there should be evidence that stored/borrowed toys or resources (e.g., cooking utensils/foods, dressing-up clothes, real or imitation musical instruments) from other cultures are sometimes used, for example, boxes of resources available for celebration of different festivals during the year, or resources representing different cultures accessible to children in the home corner. Resources representing at least two cultures other than the majority culture should be available at some time (but not necessarily daily). If no toys or resources are accessible on the day of the visit, observers should look at stored resources, and also for evidence in planning, display, and/or records that such materials are available and used.
3.2 A variety of different ethnic, cultural, and/or religious groups should be represented (e.g., at least three), and examples should be found in two of the five categories listed (i.e., books, pictures, Small World figures, dolls, and displays). If the group is diverse, photographs of the children themselves can be counted. At this level, credit can also be given for images that are tokenistic or stereotypical (e.g., other nationalities portrayed only in national dress; Africans shown only in traditional rural contexts; Black dolls with white features; books such as *Handa's Surprise* by Eileen Browne in the book selection, but no stories or pictures of African children living in Western culture). Do not give credit for images that are offensive.
5.1 To give credit for this Indicator, there should be evidence of more than occasional tokenistic celebration of other cultures/festivals (which can be credited in Indicator 3.1). Race equality and multicultural awareness should be embedded in the ethos of the center. Resources from two or more cultures should be accessible daily, and resources from at least two other cultures should be available at some time (but not necessarily daily). Planning can provide supporting evidence of the range of cultures included in day-to-day activities and celebrations.
5.2 At least three different examples should be visible/accessible daily (across at least two of the five categories).
5.3 Similarities and differences must be explicitly shown in display and/or planning. Children should receive a constant message that all children do similar everyday things (e.g., go to the park, attend weddings). Two or more examples are required in the display or planning reviewed.
5.4 If no prejudice is shown, use a question such as "What would you do if one of the children showed prejudice toward another, or made a racist remark?" Give credit for this Indicator if the answer indicates a sensitive approach: The child should not be blamed but told that their words and/or behavior are inappropriate/inaccurate. The adult should then provide a correct explanation and suggest a more appropriate response.
7.1, 7.2 These Indicators assess the extent to which staff use activities as a vehicle to take children beyond simple recognition and into understanding and respect of different races and cultures. For each Indicator, at least three explicit examples must be found in the materials reviewed (or provided as answers to questions).

The ECQRS-EC Information Sheet

Name of center ______________________________

Date of visit ____________ Time visit began ____________ Time visit ended ____________

Area(s) observed in the center

____

____

Adults: Educators and others present

____

____

Age of children observed (range and average age) ______________________________

Number of children observed on day ____________ Total number of children in observed group ____________

Total number of children who attend the center ____________

Other pertinent information (e.g., geographic area, school district, unusual event on the day)

____

____

____

____

Observer's name ______________________________

Signature ______________________________

Rough Plan of Indoor and/or Outdoor Areas Being Observed

Score Sheet

SUBSCALE 1: LANGUAGE AND EMERGENT LITERACY

Item 1: Environmental Print: Letters and Words 1 2 3 4 5 6 7

	Y	N			Y	N			Y	N			Y	N
1.1	☐	☐ D		3.1	☐	☐ D		5.1	☐	☐ D		7.1	☐	☐
1.2	☐	☐ D		3.2	☐	☐		5.2	☐	☐		7.2	☐	☐
				3.3	☐	☐ D		5.3	☐	☐		7.3	☐	☐

Item 2: Book and Literacy Areas 1 2 3 4 5 6 7

	Y	N			Y	N			Y	N			Y	N
1.1	☐	☐		3.1	☐	☐		5.1	☐	☐		7.1	☐	☐
1.2	☐	☐		3.2	☐	☐		5.2	☐	☐		7.2	☐	☐
				3.3	☐	☐						7.3	☐	☐

Item 3: Adults Reading With Children 1 2 3 4 5 6 7

	Y	N			Y	N			Y	N			Y	N
1.1	☐	☐ P, Q		3.1	☐	☐ P, Q		5.1	☐	☐		7.1	☐	☐
				3.2	☐	☐		5.2	☐	☐		7.2	☐	☐ D
												7.3	☐	☐

Item 4: Sounds in Words 1 2 3 4 5 6 7

	Y	N			Y	N			Y	N			Y	N
1.1	☐	☐ P, Q		3.1	☐	☐ P, Q		5.1	☐	☐		7.1	☐	☐ P
				3.2	☐	☐		5.2	☐	☐		7.2	☐	☐ (P)

Item 5: Emergent Writing/Mark Making

1 2 3 4 5 6 7

	Y	N			Y	N			Y	N			Y	N	
1.1	☐	☐		3.1	☐	☐		5.1	☐	☐		7.1	☐	☐	
1.2	☐	☐	D, R	3.2	☐	☐		5.2	☐	☐		7.2	☐	☐	D, R, (P)
				3.3	☐	☐	D, R	5.3	☐	☐		7.3	☐	☐	D

Item 6: Talking and Listening

1 2 3 4 5 6 7

	Y	N			Y	N			Y	N			Y	N	
1.1	☐	☐		3.1	☐	☐		5.1	☐	☐	(P)	7.1	☐	☐	
1.2	☐	☐		3.2	☐	☐		5.2	☐	☐		7.2	☐	☐	P
								5.3	☐	☐		7.3	☐	☐	
												7.4	☐	☐	

Item 7: Words and Sentences

1 2 3 4 5 6 7

	Y	N		Y	N		Y	N		Y	N
1.1	☐	☐	3.1	☐	☐	5.1	☐	☐	7.1	☐	☐
1.2	☐	☐	3.2	☐	☐	5.2	☐	☐	7.2	☐	☐
1.3	☐	☐	3.3	☐	☐	5.3	☐	☐	7.3	☐	☐
1.4	☐	☐	3.4	☐	☐	5.4	☐	☐	7.4	☐	☐

SUBSCALE 2: EMERGENT MATHEMATICS

Item 8: Counting and the Application of Counting

1 2 3 4 5 6 7

	Y	N			Y	N			Y	N			Y	N	
1.1	☐	☐	P, D, R, Q	3.1	☐	☐	P, D, R, Q	5.1	☐	☐	(P), (D), (R)	7.1	☐	☐	
1.2	☐	☐		3.2	☐	☐		5.2	☐	☐		7.2	☐	☐	P
				3.3	☐	☐	D	5.3	☐	☐		7.3	☐	☐	P
								5.4	☐	☐					

Item 9: Understanding and Representing Number 1 2 3 4 5 6 7

Y N	Y N	Y N	Y N
1.1 ☐ ☐ P, D, R	3.1 ☐ ☐ D	5.1 ☐ ☐ (P), (D), (R)	7.1 ☐ ☐ (P), (D), (R)
1.2 ☐ ☐	3.2 ☐ ☐	5.2 ☐ ☐ P, D, R	7.2 ☐ ☐ P, D, R; N/A ☐
1.3 ☐ ☐ D	3.3 ☐ ☐ D	5.3 ☐ ☐ (P), (D), (R)	

Item 10: Math Talk and Thinking Mathematically 1 2 3 4 5 6 7

Y N	Y N	Y N	Y N
1.1 ☐ ☐ P, D, R	3.1 ☐ ☐	5.1 ☐ ☐	7.1 ☐ ☐ P, D, R, Q
1.2 ☐ ☐	3.2 ☐ ☐	5.2 ☐ ☐ P, D, R	7.2 ☐ ☐ P, D, R; N/A ☐
	3.3 ☐ ☐ P, D, R, Q	5.3 ☐ ☐ P, D, R	7.3 ☐ ☐ P, D, R; N/A ☐
		5.4 ☐ ☐ Q	7.4 ☐ ☐ P, D, R, Q

Item 11a: Mathematical Activities: Shape 1 2 3 4 5 6 7

Y N	Y N	Y N	Y N
1.1 ☐ ☐ P, D, R	3.1 ☐ ☐ D	5.1 ☐ ☐	7.1 ☐ ☐ (P), (D), (R)
	3.2 ☐ ☐	5.2 ☐ ☐	7.2 ☐ ☐ P, D, R
	3.3 ☐ ☐ P, D, R		7.3 ☐ ☐ P, D, R; N/A ☐

Item 11b: Mathematical Activities: Sorting, Matching, and Comparing 1 2 3 4 5 6 7

Y N	Y N	Y N	Y N
1.1 ☐ ☐ P, D, R	3.1 ☐ ☐	5.1 ☐ ☐ (P)	7.1 ☐ ☐
	3.2 ☐ ☐ P, D, R	5.2 ☐ ☐	7.2 ☐ ☐
	3.3 ☐ ☐	5.3 ☐ ☐	7.3 ☐ ☐ P, D, R

Item 11c: Mathematical Activities: Subitizing | 1 2 3 4 5 6 7 N/A |

	Y	N			Y	N			Y	N			Y	N	
1.1	□	□	P, D, R	3.1	□	□		5.1	□	□	P, D, R	7.1	□	□	P
1.2	□	□	P, D, R	3.2	□	□		5.2	□	□	P, D, R	7.2	□	□	P, D, R
								5.3	□	□	P, D, R				

SUBSCALE 3: EMERGENT SCIENCE

Item 12: Natural Materials | 1 2 3 4 5 6 7 |

	Y	N			Y	N			Y	N			Y	N	
1.1	□	□		3.1	□	□		5.1	□	□	P, D	7.1	□	□	(P), (D)
				3.2	□	□		5.2	□	□		7.2	□	□	D, Q
								5.3	□	□		7.3	□	□	P, D, R

Item 13: Areas Featuring Science/Science Resources | 1 2 3 4 5 6 7 |

	Y	N			Y	N			Y	N			Y	N	
1.1	□	□		3.1	□	□		5.1	□	□		7.1	□	□	
				3.2	□	□	D	5.2	□	□		7.2	□	□	D
				3.3	□	□	D	5.3	□	□		7.3	□	□	
												7.4	□	□	

Item 14: Developing Scientific Thinking and the Scientific Process | 1 2 3 4 5 6 7 |

	Y	N			Y	N			Y	N			Y	N	
1.1	□	□		3.1	□	□		5.1	□	□		7.1	□	□	
1.2	□	□		3.2	□	□		5.2	□	□	P, D, R, Q	7.2	□	□	P, D, R, Q
1.3	□	□		3.3	□	□		5.3	□	□	P, D, R, Q	7.3	□	□	P, D, R, Q
1.4	□	□		3.4	□	□						For older children (4½ to 6)			
												7.4	□	□	P, D, R, Q; N/A □
												7.5	□	□	P, D, R, Q; N/A □

Item 15a: Science Activities: Nonliving **1 2 3 4 5 6 7**

	Y	N			Y	N			Y	N			Y	N	
1.1	☐	☐	P, D, R	3.1	☐	☐	P, D, R	5.1	☐	☐	P, D, R	7.1	☐	☐	(P), (D), (R)
				3.2	☐	☐	D	5.2	☐	☐		7.2	☐	☐	P, D, R
								5.3	☐	☐		7.3	☐	☐	
												7.4	☐	☐	
												7.5	☐	☐	
												7.6	☐	☐	P, D, R; N/A ☐

Item 15b: Science Activities: Living Processes **1 2 3 4 5 6 7**

	Y	N			Y	N			Y	N			Y	N	
1.1	☐	☐	P, D, R	3.1	☐	☐	P, D, R	5.1	☐	☐	P, D, R	7.1	☐	☐	(P), (D), (R)
1.2	☐	☐		3.2	☐	☐		5.2	☐	☐		7.2	☐	☐	P, D, R
				3.3	☐	☐		5.3	☐	☐		7.3	☐	☐	
				3.4	☐	☐		5.4	☐	☐		7.4	☐	☐	
												7.5	☐	☐	
												7.6	☐	☐	
												7.7	☐	☐	P, D, R; N/A ☐

Item 15c: Science Activities: Food Preparation **1 2 3 4 5 6 7 N/A**

	Y	N			Y	N			Y	N			Y	N	
1.1	☐	☐	P, D, R, Q	3.1	☐	☐	P, D, R, Q	5.1	☐	☐	P, D, R, Q	7.1	☐	☐	P
1.2	☐	☐		3.2	☐	☐	P, D, Q	5.2	☐	☐	P, D, R, Q	7.2	☐	☐	
				3.3	☐	☐		5.3	☐	☐		7.3	☐	☐	
				3.4	☐	☐		5.4	☐	☐		7.4	☐	☐	
								5.5	☐	☐					

SUBSCALE 4: SUPPORTING DIVERSITY AND INCLUSION

Item 16: Planning for and Supporting Individual Learning Needs **1 2 3 4 5 6 7**

	Y	N			Y	N			Y	N			Y	N	
1.1	☐	☐	P, Q	3.1	☐	☐	P, Q	5.1	☐	☐	P, Q	7.1	☐	☐	Q
1.2	☐	☐	P	3.2	☐	☐	P	5.2	☐	☐	P	7.2	☐	☐	P
1.3	☐	☐	P	3.3	☐	☐	R	5.3	☐	☐	R	7.3	☐	☐	P, R, Q
1.4	☐	☐	R	3.4	☐	☐		5.4	☐	☐	(D)	7.4	☐	☐	P, D, R
				3.5	☐	☐	D	5.5	☐	☐	Q	7.5	☐	☐	Q

Item 17: Gender Equality and Awareness **1 2 3 4 5 6 7**

	Y	N			Y	N			Y	N			Y	N	
1.1	☐	☐	D	3.1	☐	☐	D	5.1	☐	☐	D	7.1	☐	☐	P, Q
1.2	☐	☐		3.2	☐	☐		5.2	☐	☐	(Q)	7.2	☐	☐	Q
				3.3	☐	☐		5.3	☐	☐	(P), (Q)	7.3	☐	☐	Q

Item 18: Race Equality and Awareness **1 2 3 4 5 6 7**

	Y	N			Y	N			Y	N			Y	N	
1.1	☐	☐	D	3.1	☐	☐	P, D, R	5.1	☐	☐	(P)	7.1	☐	☐	P, D, R, Q
1.2	☐	☐	D	3.2	☐	☐	D	5.2	☐	☐	D	7.2	☐	☐	P, D, R, Q
1.3	☐	☐	N/A ☐					5.3	☐	☐	P, D	7.3	☐	☐	Q
								5.4	☐	☐					

Joint Observation/Inter-Rater Reliability for the ECQRS-EC

Center observed ______________________________ Date ______________

Group of children/room ______________ Adults, educators, or others present ______________

Observers ______________________________

Subscales and Items	Observer 1	Observer 2	Observer 3	Observer 4	Agreed final score
Subscale 1: Language and Emergent Literacy					
Item 1: Environmental print: Letters and words					
Item 2: Book and literacy areas					
Item 3: Adults reading with children					
Item 4: Sounds in words					
Item 5: Emergent writing/mark making					
Item 6: Talking and listening					
Item 7: Words and sentences					
Subscale 2: Emergent Mathematics					
Item 8: Counting and the application of counting					
Item 9: Understanding and representing number					
Item 10: Math talk and thinking mathematically					
Item 11a: Mathematical activities: Shape					
Item 11b: Mathematical activities: Sorting, matching, and comparing					
Item 11c: Mathematical activities: Subitizing					
Subscale 3: Emergent Science					
Item 12: Natural materials					
Item 13: Areas featuring science/science resources					
Item 14: Developing scientific thinking and the scientific process					
Item 15a: Science activities: Nonliving					
Item 15b: Science activities: Living processes					
Item 15c: Science activities: Food preparation					
Subscale 4: Supporting Diversity and Inclusion					
Item 16: Planning for and supporting individual learning needs					
Item 17: Gender equality and awareness					
Item 18: Race equality and awareness					

ECQRS-EC Profile

Subscale 1: Language and Emergent Literacy											
Obs 1	Obs 2	Obs 3	Average Subscale score	1	2	3	4	5	6	7	Item 1: Environmental print: Letters and words
Obs 1	Obs 2	Obs 3		1	2	3	4	5	6	7	Item 2: Book and literacy areas
Obs 1	Obs 2	Obs 3		1	2	3	4	5	6	7	Item 3: Adults reading with children
Obs 1	Obs 2	Obs 3		1	2	3	4	5	6	7	Item 4: Sounds in words
Obs 1	Obs 2	Obs 3		1	2	3	4	5	6	7	Item 5: Emergent writing/mark making
Obs 1	Obs 2	Obs 3		1	2	3	4	5	6	7	Item 6: Talking and listening
Obs 1	Obs 2	Obs 3		1	2	3	4	5	6	7	Item 7: Words and sentences

Subscale 2: Emergent Mathematics											
Obs 1	Obs 2	Obs 3	Average Subscale score	1	2	3	4	5	6	7	Item 8: Counting and the application of counting
Obs 1	Obs 2	Obs 3		1	2	3	4	5	6	7	Item 9: Understanding and representing number
Obs 1	Obs 2	Obs 3		1	2	3	4	5	6	7	Item 10: Math talk and thinking mathematically
Obs 1	Obs 2	Obs 3		1	2	3	4	5	6	7	Item 11a: Mathematical activities: Shape
Obs 1	Obs 2	Obs 3		1	2	3	4	5	6	7	Item 11b: Mathematical activities: Sorting, matching, and comparing
Obs 1	Obs 2	Obs 3		1	2	3	4	5	6	7	Item 11c: Mathematical activities: Subitizing

Subscale 3: Emergent Science											
Obs 1	Obs 2	Obs 3	Average Subscale score	1	2	3	4	5	6	7	Item 12: Natural materials
Obs 1	Obs 2	Obs 3		1	2	3	4	5	6	7	Item 13: Areas featuring science/science resources
Obs 1	Obs 2	Obs 3		1	2	3	4	5	6	7	Item 14: Developing scientific thinking and the scientific process
Obs 1	Obs 2	Obs 3		1	2	3	4	5	6	7	Item 15a: Science activities: Nonliving
Obs 1	Obs 2	Obs 3		1	2	3	4	5	6	7	Item 15b: Science activities: Living processes
Obs 1	Obs 2	Obs 3		1	2	3	4	5	6	7	Item 15c: Science activities: Food preparation

Subscale 4: Supporting Diversity and Inclusion											
Obs 1	Obs 2	Obs 3	Average Subscale score	1	2	3	4	5	6	7	Item 16: Planning for and supporting individual learning needs
Obs 1	Obs 2	Obs 3		1	2	3	4	5	6	7	Item 17: Gender equality and awareness
Obs 1	Obs 2	Obs 3		1	2	3	4	5	6	7	Item 18: Race equality and awareness

References

Adams, M. J. (1990). Beginning to read: Thinking and learning. *Psychological Review, 65*, 197–208.

Agogi, E., Rossis, D., & Stylianidou, F. (2014). *Creative Little Scientists: Set of recommendations to policy makers and stakeholders. Deliverable D6.6* (p. 64). EU Project FP7 (Contract: SIS-CP-2011-289081; Project Coordinator: Ellinogermaniki Agogi, Greece). Retrieved April 2023 from http://www.creative-little-scientists.eu/content/deliverables

Anders, Y., Grosse, C., Rossbach, H. G., Ebert, S., & Weinert, S. (2013). Preschool and primary school influences on the development of children's early numeracy skills between the ages of 3 and 7 years in Germany. *School Effectiveness and School Improvement, 24*(2), 195–211.

Anders, Y., Rossbach, H. G., Weinert, S., Ebert, S., Kuger, S., Lehrl, S., & Von Maurice, J. (2012). Home and preschool learning environments and their relations to the development of early numeracy skills. *Early Childhood Research Quarterly, 27*(2), 231–244.

Archer, C., & Siraj, I. (2017). *Movement Environment Rating Scale (MOVERS) for 2–6-year-olds provision: Improving physical development through movement and physical activity*. Trentham Books & UCL-IoE Press.

Archer, C., & Siraj, I. (2024). *Movement Environment Rating Scale (MOVERS): Supporting physical development and movement play in early childhood*. Routledge.

Baroody, A. (1987). *Children's mathematical thinking: A developmental framework for preschool, primary, and special education teachers*. Teachers College Press.

Bowman, M., & Treiman, R. (2004). Stepping stones to reading. *Theory into Practice, 43*(4), 295–303.

Burchinal, M. R., Peisner-Feinberg, E., Pianta, R., & Howes, C. (2002). Development of academic skills from preschool through second grade: Family and classroom predictors of developmental trajectories. *Journal of School Psychology, 40*(5), 415–436.

Burger, K. (2010). How does early childhood care and education affect cognitive development? An international review of the effects of early interventions for children from different social backgrounds. *Early Childhood Research Quarterly, 25*(2), 140–165.

Carey, S., & Smith, C. (1993). On understanding the nature of scientific knowledge. *Educational Psychologist, 28*(3), 235–251.

Clay, M. M. (1993). *An observation survey of early literacy achievement*. Heinemann.

Clements, D. H., & Sarama, J. (2014). *Learning and teaching early math. The learning trajectories approach* (2nd ed.). Routledge.

Clements, D. H., & Sarama, J. (2017/2019). *Learning and teaching with learning trajectories [LT]2*. Marsico Institute, Morgridge College of Education, University of Denver.

Day, C., & Sammons, P. (2020). *Successful school leadership*. Education Development Trust. https://www.educationdevelopmenttrust.com

Duncan, G. J., & Magnuson, K. (2013). Investing in preschool programs. *Journal of Economic Perspectives, 27*(2), 109–132.

Education Endowment Foundation. (2020–2022). *The impact of COVID 19 on school starters*. London Education Endowment Fund.

Epstein, A. S. (2014). *The intentional teacher. Choosing the best strategies for young children's learning* (Rev. ed.). HighScope Press.

Glauert, E., Trakulphadetkrai, N., & Maloney, J. [Lead Authors]. (2013). *Creative Little Scientists: Report on practices and their implications. Deliverable D4.4*. EU Project FP7 (Contract: SIS-CP-2011-289081; Project Coordinator: Ellinogermanik Agogi, Greece). Retrieved April 2023 from http://www.creative-little-scientists.eu/content/deliverables

Gopnik, A., Meltzoff, A. N., & Kuhl, P. K. (1999). *The scientist in the crib: Minds, brains, and how children learn*. William Morrow.

Hall, J., Sylva, K., Melhuish, E., Sammons, P., Siraj-Blatchford, I., & Taggart, B. (2009). The role of pre-school quality in promoting resilience in the cognitive development of young children. *Oxford Review of Education, 35*(3), 331–352.

Harms, T., Clifford, R. M., & Cryer, D. (2014). *Early Childhood Environment Rating Scale (ECERS-3)* (3rd ed.). Teachers College Press.

Harms, T., Clifford, R. M., & Cryer, D. (2004). *Early Childhood Environment Rating Scale (ECERS-R)* (rev. ed.). Teachers College Press.

Harms, T., Cryer, D., Clifford, R. M., & Yazejian, N. (2017). *Infant/Toddler Environment Rating Scale (ITERS-3)* (3rd ed.). Teachers College Press. [Previously Harms, T., Cryer, D., & Clifford, R. M. (2007). *Infant/Toddler Environment Rating Scale (ITERS-R)* (rev. ed.). Teachers College Press.]

Harms, T., Cryer, D., Clifford, R. M., & Yazejian, N. (2019). *Family Child Care Environment Rating Scale (FCCERS-3)* (3rd ed.). Teachers College Press. [Previously Harms, T., Cryer, D., & Clifford, R. M. (2007). *Family Child Care Environment Rating Scale (FCCERS-R)* (rev. ed.). Teachers College Press.]

Harms, T., Vineberg Jacobs, E., & Romano White, D. (2015). *School-Age Care Environment Rating Scale (SACERS-R)* (rev. ed.). Teachers College Press.

HighScope (2018) The emotional backpack: managing conflict resolution with children of trauma. https://highscope.org/wp-content/uploads/2018/11/HSActiveLearner_2018Fall_sample.pdf.

Huang, R., & Siraj, I. (2023). Profiles of Chinese preschoolers' academic and social–emotional development in relation to classroom quality: A multilevel latent profile approach. *Child Development, 94*(4), 1002–1016. https://doi.org/10.1111/cdev.13916

IOE—Faculty of Education. (2024). *EPPSE publications*. University College London. https://www.ucl.ac.uk/ioe/research/featured-research/eppse-publications

Justice, L. M., & Ezell, H. K. (2001). Word and print awareness in 4-year-old children. *Child Language Teaching and Therapy, 17*(3), 207–225.

Justice, L. M., & Kaderavek, J. H. (2002). Using shared storybook reading to promote emergent literacy. *Teaching Exceptional Children, 34*(4), 8–13.

Justice, L. M., & Pullen, P. C. (2003). Promising interventions for promoting emergent literacy skills: Three evidence-based approaches. *Topics in Early Childhood Special Education, 23*(3), 99–113. https://doi.org/10.1177/02711214030230030101

Klieme, E., Funke, J., Leutner, D., Reimann, P., & Wirth, J. (2001). Problemlösen als fächerübergreifende Kompetenz. Konzeption und erste Resultate aus einer Schulleistungsstudie [Problem solving as crosscurricular competency. Conception and first results out of a school performance study]. *Zeitschrift für Pädagogik, 47*, 179–200.

Lehrl, S., Kluczniok, K., & Rossbach, H. G. (2016). Longer-term associations of preschool education: The predictive role of preschool quality for the development of mathematical skills through elementary school. *Early Childhood Research Quarterly, 36*, 475–488.

Leithwood, K. (2017). The Ontario Leadership Framework: Successful school leadership practices and personal leadership resources. In K. Leithwood, J. Sun, & K. Pollock (Eds.), *How school leaders contribute to student success: The four paths framework* (pp. 31–43). Springer.

Lesh, R., Post, T., & Behr, M. (1987). Representation and translations among representations in mathematics learning and problem solving. In C. Janvier (Ed.), *Problems of representations in the teaching and learning of mathematics* (pp. 33–40). Erlbaum.

Magnuson, K. A., Kelchen, R., Duncan, G. J., Schindler, H. S., Shager, H., & Yoshikawa, H. (2016). Do the effects of early childhood education programs differ by gender? A meta-analysis. *Early Childhood Research Quarterly, 36*, 521–536.

Mann, V. A., & Foy, J. G. (2003). Phonological awareness, speech development, and letter knowledge in preschool children. *Annals of Dyslexia, 53*, 149–173.

Masters, A. S., Scott, M. E., Wright, C. A., Toub, T. S., Dickinson, D. K., Golinkoff, R. M., & Hirsh-Pasek, K. (2023). Playing with words: Using playful learning experiences in the early childhood classroom to build vocabulary. *The Reading Teacher, 76*(6), 775–783.

Mayer, R. E., & Wittrock, M. C. (1996). Problem-solving transfer. In D. C. Berliner & R. C. Calfee (Eds.), *Handbook of educational psychology* (pp. 47–62). Macmillan.

Melhuish, E. C., Ereky-Stevens, K., Petrogiannis, K., Ariescu, A., Penderi, E., Rentzou, K., & Leserman, P. (2015). *A review of research on the effects of Early Childhood Education and Care (ECEC) on child development. CARE project.* Curriculum Quality Analysis and Impact Review of European Early Childhood Education and Care (ECEC).

Melhuish, E., & Gardiner, J. (2023). *Equal hours? The impact of hours spent in early years provision on children's outcomes at age five, by socio-economic background.* Sutton Trust. https://www.suttontrust.com/wp-content/uploads/2023/01/Equal-Hours.pdf

Merttens, R. (2012). The "concrete-pictorial-abstract" heuristic. *Mathematics Teaching, 228*, 33–38.

Norway Ministry of Education and Research. (2023). *Early childhood education and care.* Retrieved May 2024 from https://www.regjeringen.no/en/topics/families-and-children/kindergarden/early-childhood-education-and-care-polic/id491283/

Nunes, T., & Bryant, P. (1996). *Children doing mathematics.* Wiley Blackwell.

OECD. (2022). *Improving early equity: From evidence to action.* Retrieved April 2023 from https://doi.org/10.1787/6eff314c-en

Pascal, C., Bertram, T., Cullinane, C., & Holt-White, E. (2020). *COVID-19 and social mobility Impact Brief #4: Early years.* Sutton Trust. Retrieved April 2023 from https://www.suttontrust.com/wp-content/uploads/2020/06/Early-Years-Impact-Brief.pdf

Reys, R., Lindquist, M., Lambdin, D., & Smith, N. (2012). *Helping children learn mathematics* (10th ed.). Wiley.

Rossis, D., & Stylianidou, F. [Lead Authors]. (2014). *Creative Little Scientists: Set of recommendations to policy makers and stakeholders. Deliverable 6.6.* EU Project FP7 (Contract: SIS-CP-2011-289081; Project Coordinator: Ellinogermaniki Agogi, Greece). Retrieved April 2023 from http://www.creative-little-scientists.eu/content/deliverables

Sammons, P., Gu, Q., Day, C., & Ko, J. (2011). Exploring the impact of school leadership on pupil outcomes: Results from a study of academically improved and effective schools in England. *International Journal of Educational Management, 25*(1), 83–101. [Emerald Literati Outstanding Paper Award 2012, *International Journal of Educational Management.*]

Sammons, P., Sylva, K., Melhuish, E. C., Siraj, I., Taggart, B., & Hunt, S. (2008). *The Effective Pre-School and Primary Education 3–11 Project (EPPE 3–11). Influences on children's attainment and progress in key stage 2: Cognitive outcomes in Year 6.* DCSF/Institute of Education, University of London. https://dera.ioe.ac.uk/id/eprint/18190/1/DCSF-RR048.pdf

Siraj, I., & Kingston, D. (in press). *The Pedagogical Leadership in the Early Years (PLEY) Scale.* Routledge.

Siraj, I., Kingston, D., & Melhuish, E. (2015). *Assessing quality: Sustained Shared Thinking and Emotional Well-Being (SSTEW) rating scale.* Trentham Books & UCL-IoE Press.

Siraj, I., Kingston, D., & Melhuish, E. (2024). *The Sustained Shared Thinking and Emotional Well-Being (SSTEW) scale: Supporting process quality in early childhood.* Routledge.

Siraj, I., Melhuish, E., Howard, S. J., Neilsen-Hewett, C., Kingston, D., De Rosnay, M., Huang, R., Gardiner, J., & Luu, B. (2023). Improving quality of teaching and child development: A randomised controlled trial of the leadership for learning intervention in preschools. *Frontiers in Psychology, 13*, 1092284. Retrieved April 2023 from https://www.frontiersin.org/articles/10.3389/fpsyg.2022.1092284/full

Siraj-Blatchford, I., Sylva, K., Gilden, R., Muttock, S., & Bell, D. (2002). *Effective Pedagogy in the Early Years (REPEY).* Research Report 356, Department for Education and Employment. Retrieved April 2023 from https://dera.ioe.ac.uk/4650/1/RR356.pdf

Siraj-Blatchford, I., Sylva, K., Taggart. B., Sammons, P., Melhuish, E. & Elliot, K. (2003) *The effective provision of pre-school education (EPPE) project: Technical Paper 10.* Intensive Case Studies of Practice Across the Foundation Stage. DfEE/Institute of Education.

Snow, C. E. (1991). The theoretical basis for relationships between language and literacy in development. *Journal of Research in Childhood Education, 6*(1), 5–10. https://doi.org/10.1080/02568549109594817

Snow, C., Burns, M. S., & Griffin, P. (1999). Language and literacy environments in preschools. *ERIC Digests*, ED426818.

Sylva, K., Melhuish, E. C., Sammons, P., Siraj, I., & Taggart, B. (2008). *Final report from the primary phase: Pre-school, school and family influences on children's development during key stage 2 (7–11)* (DCSF Research Report 61). Institute of Education, University of London. https://dera.ioe.ac.uk/id/eprint/8543/1/Final%203-11%20report%20DfE-RR061%2027nov08.pdf

Sylva, K., Melhuish, E., Sammons, P., Siraj-Blatchford, I., & Taggart, B. (2010). *Early childhood.* Routledge.

Sylva, K., Sammons, P., Melhuish, E. C., Siraj, I., & Taggart, B. (2020). Developing 21st century skills in early childhood: The contribution of process quality to self-regulation and pro-social behaviour. *Zeitschrift für Erziehungswissenschaft, 23*(3).

Sylva, K., Siraj, I., Melhuish, E. C., Sammons, P., Taggart, B., Evans, E., Dobson, A., Jeavons, M., Lewis, K., Morahan, M., & Sadler, S. (1999). *The Effective Provision of Pre-School Education (EPPE) Project: Technical Paper 6. Characteristics of the centres in the EPPE sample: Observational profiles.* Institute of Education, University of London. https://dera.ioe.ac.uk/id/eprint/18189/8/EPPE_TechnicalPaper_06_1999.pdf

Sylva, K., Siraj-Blatchford, I., & Taggart, B. (2011). *ECERS-E: The four curricular subscales extension to the Early Childhood Environment Rating Scale (ECERS-R).* Teachers College Press. (Original work published 2003)

Sylva, K., Siraj-Blatchford, I., Taggart, B., Sammons, P., Melhuish, E., Elliot, K., & Totsika, V. (2006). Capturing quality in early childhood through environmental rating scales. *Early Childhood Research Quarterly, 21*(1), 76–92.

Sylva, K., Taggart, B., Siraj-Blatchford, I., Totsika, V., Ereky-Stevens, K., Gilden, R., & Bell, D. (2007). Curricular quality and day-to-day learning activities in pre-school. *International Journal of Early Years Education, 15*(1), 49–65. https://doi.org/10.1080/09669760601106968

Taggart, B. (2010). Making a difference: How research can inform policy. In K. Sylva, E. Melhuish, P. Sammons, I. Siraj-Blatchford, & B. Taggart (Eds.), *Early childhood matters: Evidence from the Effective Pre-school and Primary Education Project* (Chapter 11). Routledge.

Taggart, B., Sylva, K., Melhuish, E., Sammons, P., & Siraj, I. (2015). *Effective Pre-school, Primary and Secondary Education Project (EPPSE 3–16+): How pre-school influences children and young people's attainment and developmental outcomes over time* (Research Brief, Ref. DFE-RB455). Department for Education. https://assets.publishing.service.gov.uk/government/uploads/system/uploads/attachment_data/file/455670/RB455_Effective_pre-school_primary_and_secondary_education_project.pdf.pdf

Thorpe, K., Rankin, P., Houen, S., Beatton, T., Sandi, M., Siraj, I., & Staton, S. (2020). The when and what of measuring ECE quality: Analysis of variation in the Classroom Assessment Scoring System (CLASS) across the ECE day. *Early Childhood Research Quarterly, 53*(4), 274–286. https://doi.org/10.1016/j.ecresq.2020.05.003

Van de Walle, J. A., Lovin, L. H., Karp, K. S., & Bay-Williams, J. M. (2018). *Teaching student-centered mathematics. Developmentally appropriate instruction for grades preK–2* (3rd ed., Vol. 1). Pearson.

Walker, A., & Hallinger, P. (2015). Systematic reviews of research on principal leadership in East Asia. *Journal of Educational Administration, 53*(4), 554–570.

Welsch, J. G., Sullivan, A., & Justice, L. M. (2003). That's my letter: What preschoolers' name writing representations tell us about emergent literacy knowledge. *Journal of Literacy Research, 35*(2), 757–776.

World Economic Forum Annual Meeting (2016). https://www.weforum.org/events/world-economic-forum-annual-meeting-2016/

Notes